Administrative Law
for the
Construction Industry

ADMINISTRATIVE LAW FOR THE CONSTRUCTION INDUSTRY

J. R. Lewis
LL.B., A.C.I.S. of the
Inner Temple, Barrister-at-law

M

First published 1976 by
THE MACMILLAN PRESS LTD
London and Basingstoke
Associated companies in New York Dublin
Melbourne Johannesburg and Madras

SBN 333 18049 6 (hard cover)
333 18590 0 (paper cover)

Produced by computer-controlled phototypesetting,
using OCR input techniques, and printed offset by
UNWIN BROTHERS LIMITED
The Gresham Press, Old Woking, Surrey

Contents

Preface

The construction industry has had to face during the last few years a considerable amount of change as far as the law relating to its activities in the public sector is concerned. The Local Government Act 1972 reshaped the structure of local authorities and reallocated functions; further changes came in as a result of the 1974 Act, and new controls emerged through the Town and Country Amenities Act 1974, the Health and Safety at Work Act 1974, the Control of Pollution Act 1974, and the Housing Rents and Subsidies Act 1975.

These Acts, the Community Land Act 1975, and other relevant changes by way of court cases and statutory instruments, are dealt with in this book, which is designed for students preparing for the Administrative Law paper in the Final Examination of the Royal Institution of Chartered Surveyors ('General Practice' and 'Quantity Surveying'). It should also prove useful for all others who work in the construction industry and for whom a knowledge of administrative law is necessary, such as architects and civil engineers.

Table of Cases

Table of Statutes

1

The Organisation of Local Government

In 1971 a consultative document covering Wales and a White Paper – 'Local Government in England: Government Proposals for Reorganisation' – created the base from which was enacted in 1972 the Local Government Act. The 1972 legislation swept away an out-dated system of local authorities and created new structures. The Act allocated functions among these new authorities and modified the administration within the local authorities. While it did not materially affect the working of London government, since this had been modified by the London Government Act 1963, it replaced the Local Government Act 1933 and incorporated the provisions of the 1963 Act affecting the constitution of authorities in Greater London.

The effect of the 1972 Act was that England (outside Greater London) and Wales were divided administratively into counties and districts. Some of the English counties were designated 'metropolitan counties', with districts within them named 'metropolitan districts'. Otherwise, districts in England were divided into parishes; in Wales, into communities. Counties, districts, Greater London and the London boroughs are called 'principal areas'; their councils are called 'principal councils'.

For historical reasons and matters of local pride many districts still call themselves 'boroughs', with borough councils, while some parishes style themselves 'towns' and have town councils. There are also some areas which were formerly cities or boroughs and which have bodies called the 'charter trustees' of the city or of the town.

AREAS AND STATUS

The Local Government Act 1972 divided England (other than Greater London) and Wales into 53 counties and 369 districts. Six of the 53 counties are metropolitan counties containing all together 36 metropolitan districts. Where rural parishes existed before 1 April 1974 they continue as parishes; rural boroughs (created by the Local Government Act 1958, s. 28) become parishes. Each parish must have a parish meeting; small parishes may, large parishes must, have a parish council. Several parishes may group under a common council. Districts in Wales are divided into communities (formerly the boroughs, urban districts and rural parishes); parishes existing before 1 April 1974 have become community councils; boroughs or urban district councils could apply before 1973 to the Secretary of State for an order creating a community council for the area. District councils must establish community councils if the community meeting so resolves; a community council must be dissolved if the meeting so requests.

The status of the borough did not disappear with the 1972 Act, nor was the door to such status closed, for by section 245 a district council may petition the Queen for a charter conferring upon the district the status of borough. Where the charter is granted by the Privy Council the district council becomes a borough council and its chairman becomes mayor, its vice-chairman deputy mayor. Councils of parishes or communities can become 'towns' by so resolving, and a simple majority will suffice.

It should be noted that the 1972 Act effectively abolished boroughs and cities as units of government. Nevertheless the charters were not abrogated and so the rights and privileges accorded to the status were preserved. It follows that in many former cities and boroughs the offices of sheriff, high steward, recorder and honorary freemen remain unaffected. A continuation of the titles formerly bestowed on mayors of cities or royal boroughs – such as 'the right honourable' or 'the right worshipful' – is possible by Letters Patent conferred by the Queen on the advice of the Secretary of State for Home Affairs.

Reviews of Areas and Status

The task of carrying out reviews of local government areas falls upon the two Local Government Boundary Commissions and the district councils themselves.

The Commissions. The Local Government Boundary Commission for England is a body corporate consisting of a chairman, deputy chairman and not more than five members. It is an advisory body empowered to make recommendations to the Secretary of State; its duty is to undertake a regular review of certain areas[1] at not less than ten-year intervals and not more than fifteen-year intervals. The interval can be varied by the Secretary of State. Between periodic reviews the Commission can carry out an *ad hoc* review of an area and in the case of non-metropolitan districts the duty is an on-going one: no interval timings are stated. Local authorities or parish meetings may ask the Commission to undertake a review.

The Secretary of State retains certain powers of control of the Commission's work in that he can direct the holding, making, or postponement of reviews.

In making its review the Commission must have in mind 'the interests of effective and convenient local government' and can recommend a number of steps, or combination of steps, in formulating its proposals. It may advise:

(*a*) the alteration of an area;

(*b*) creation of a new area by amalgamation (outside Greater London);

(*c*) abolition of a principal area outside Greater London;

(*d*) conversion of a metropolitan into a non-metropolitan county, or vice versa, with consequent changes in status of the districts within;

(*e*) constitution of a new London borough by an amalgamation;

(*f*) abolition of a London borough and distribution of its area;

(*g*) constitution of a new parish;

(*h*) abolition of a parish.

It cannot propose the conversion of a metropolitan into a non-metropolitan county, or vice versa, without first carrying out a review. Where a review has been completed the Commission reports to the Secretary of State and makes its recommendation. The Secretary of State cannot act upon the report until six weeks have passed so that time for objections is possible. He may then make an order regarding the recommendations, with or without modifications. The order will be by way of statutory instrument; if it modifies the Commission's recommendations the Secretary of State may ask for a further review or revision of proposals. Either House of Parliament can negative his order where he alters the area of an authority other than a parish, or abolishes an authority other than a parish.

The Commission may receive guidance from the Secretary of State, but where he directs a review of all or any of the principal areas in England he must first have consulted the local authority associations.

The Local Government Boundary Commission for Wales is, like its

English counterpart, a corporate body but differs in that it has only three members apart from chairman and deputy chairman and one of the members must be Welsh-speaking. Its first task was to review Wales so as to make changes in areas, councils and electoral arrangements of communities, counties and districts. Schedule 10 of the 1972 Act gave the Commission power to alter a community, constitute new communities by amalgamation, abolish a community and distribute its area among other communities, add to community areas and alter the area of a county or district in consequence of such changes made separately or in combination.

It has in addition a continuing duty to keep the Welsh counties and districts under review, without specified periods being laid down. Directions can be given by the Secretary of State for Wales but he cannot direct that the review should not be held within a specified period. Otherwise he may give guidance and must, like his English counterpart, consult appropriate local authority associations before directing reviews affecting the principal areas in Wales.

Section 54 of the Act empowers the Welsh Commission to make proposals for change to the Secretary of State for Wales in respect of local government areas and communities along the lines outlined above.

The District Councils. Apart from the reviews carried out by the Commissions the district councils themselves have a duty to keep under review the whole of their areas, to consider whether or not proposals should be made to the English Commission for the constitution of new parishes, or the abolition or alteration of existing parishes. The district council may be asked to make a review by the parish council; by section 48 of the Act it must then do so unless it considers the review would impede the proper discharge of its reviewing functions generally.

When a review has been completed the district submits a report to the Commission, which may then make proposals to the Secretary of State, with or without modification. It may, on the other hand, undertake its own review if it considers the district proposals are not suitable for securing effective and convenient local government or where the district has reported that it will not recommend action.

In Wales the same duty falls upon the councils of the districts, to consider recommendations for the constitution of new communities, or the abolition or alteration of existing communities.

Procedure. Certain steps must be followed whether the Commission or district council is working in England or Wales. The object of the procedure is to ensure that interested parties are informed of the situation and are able to make representations concerning the review. Thus:

(1) local authorities whose areas are affected must be consulted, as must other local authorities and public bodies who would appear to be concerned;

(2) consultations with bodies representing staff employed by local authorities asking to be consulted must be undertaken;

(3) persons interested in the review must be informed of draft proposals and recommendations and of the place where the relevant documents may be inspected;

(4) the final decision taken by the Commission or council must take account of representations made.

Consultation with other councils of local government areas affected may be made by the Commission after recommendations have been made by a district council following a review; where the Commission or district council decides to hold an enquiry it may do so, with provisions for subpoena, penalties for failure to attend, and the award of costs, applying.

Where alteration of boundaries between England and Welsh counties are contemplated the proposed review must be properly publicised, as must the draft proposals. These must be available for public inspection, objections must be received if any arise and a local enquiry held if the Commission(s) think(s) fit.

Reviews of Electoral Areas

The initial electoral areas after 1972 were designated by the Secretary of State for Home Affairs, but Part IV of the Local Government Act 1972 laid down permanent machinery for the review of these areas, through the agency of the Local Government Commissions for England and Wales.

Both Commissions were required to carry out reviews of the initial electoral areas as soon as practicable after the first district council elections in England and as soon as practicable after 1 April 1974 in Wales with respect to a special community review. But a duty was also imposed upon the Commissions to take a longer-term view of the situations: thus, periodic reviews must be carried out to make proposals for necessary changes in local electoral areas, at intervals of not less than ten nor more than fifteen years. The Commissions may be requested by persons or authorities to carry out reviews at any time, however.

When the review is completed the Commission must report to the Secretary of State with its recommendations; he may make an order with or without modifications.

The district councils are under a similar duty to review the electoral arrangements of the parishes within their boundaries, and make appropriate orders. The review can be initiated by a request from at least thirty electors in the parish; where thirty such electors make a request to the Commission it may send recommendations to the district council who may make an order as recommended, or with such modifications as are acceptable to the Commission. In the event of a disagreement, the Commission may make its own proposals direct to the Secretary of State, as it may where the district council defaults in the making of a recommended order.

By section 78 of the 1972 Act these alterations are described as 'substantial changes', i.e. changes in electoral arrangements for a local government area which are independent of changes in the *boundaries* of that area.

Schedule 11 of the Act lays down the rules to be followed in considering electoral arrangements.

(*a*) In the counties the number of electors in electoral divisions must be roughly the same.

(*b*) Electoral divisions may not be split between districts and parishes.

(*c*) Communities must not be split as between electoral divisions.

(*d*) Numbers of electors per councillor in the wards of London boroughs and districts must be roughly the same.

(*e*) In parishes and communities wards cannot be introduced until it is decided that the number and distribution of electors is such as to make a single election of councillors practicable or convenient, and it is desirable that areas be separately represented on the council.

ADMINISTRATIVE MACHINERY

The work of the local authorities is carried out, on a policy-making basis, by councils and committees of the authority. Principal councils comprise a chairman and councillors; the chairman is elected annually from among the councillors, who must also appoint a vice-chairman, and reasonable expenses are payable to cover the expense of office. It was held in *Attorney-General v. Blackburn Corporation* (1887) that the power to make such an allowance must be exercised in good faith.

Parish councils are made up of a chairman and council members, but while an allowance may be paid to the chairman it is not payable to the vice-chairman, who may be appointed from among the members.

The use of committees to transact the business of authorities, by way of delegation from the councils, is a practice of some antiquity and by sections 101 and 102 of the 1972 Act authorities may appoint committees as they think fit. In some cases, however, they *must* appoint committees: the education committee is a case in point, as is the social services committee,[2] and the police committee.[3] In situations where a committee is mandatory an authority can act without proceeding through that committee only in cases of extreme urgency, though it may in fact give an officer power to carry out the function of the committee in question.

Council Members

The members of councils have no executive powers in their individual right and are unable to exercise personal lawful authority – they act only in a corporate way. Even so, standing orders will often grant members certain qualified rights – the inspection of land owned by the authority for instance – and in some instances uncodified practices are such that the chairman of a committee may be customarily empowered to make approvals between the times that his committee meets.

A number of legal rights and duties have been imposed upon and granted to council members by common law and by statute. The principal common law right of the council member concerns his right to inspect such documents as are reasonably necessary to allow him to carry out his duties as a member. In *R. v. Barnes Borough Council,* ex p. *Conlan* (1938) a councillor demanded to see the draft case prepared by counsel where he opposed the authority's decision to defend an action at law: it was held he should be denied such access for inspection was inspired by an indirect motive. The proper way to enforce the right is by way of the order of mandamus.

Other specific rights and duties are as follows:

Disclosure of Interest. Sections 94 to 98 of the Local Government Act 1972 provide that if a member has a direct or indirect pecuniary interest in any contract or proposed contract or other matter, and is present at the meeting when it is discussed, he must declare his interest and must not vote. The standing orders of authorities usually state that such members should be excluded from the meeting, subject to the majority of members present deciding otherwise. But what is meant by an 'indirect' interest?

A member will have an indirect interest if he or his nominee is a member of a body contracting with the authority, or about to do so, or which has a direct pecuniary interest in the matter being considered. Equally, he will have an indirect interest if he is a partner of, or employed by, a person with whom the contract is made or is proposed to be made, or who has a direct pecuniary interest in the matter under consideration. But there is *no* 'indirect' interest where the employee or member works for a public body, nor is the interest of one married person deemed to be that of his or her spouse. The indirect pecuniary interest may arise from a man's beneficial interest in securities held by himself or his wife; in such cases, if the total nominal value of the shares in question does not exceed £1000 (or one-hundredth of the total nominal value of the issued share capital, whichever is the less) then the member must declare his interest, but *can* speak and vote on the matter before the council.

What is the situation where the interest is of a trifling or insignificant nature? The principle of *de minimis non curat lex* had no application to the interest provisions, but by the Local Government (Pecuniary Interests) Act 1964, the rule was effectively applied. Section 97(5) of the 1972 Act re-enacts the principle and states that an interest which is so remote or insignificant that it could not reasonably be regarded as likely to influence a member in discussion and voting shall not be treated as a pecuniary interest disbarring him from speaking and voting. It excludes, additionally, an interest which a member may have as a ratepayer, inhabitant of the area or water consumer or as a person entitled to take part in any service offered to the public.

In the application of the rule the courts have drawn a distinction between pecuniary *interest* and pecuniary *advantage*. In *Brown v. Director of Public Prosecutions* (1956) six members who were tenants voted against a motion which, effectively, meant they were voting to place themselves at a specific pecuniary disadvantage. They were found guilty of an offence in so voting and when on appeal they claimed they had no pecuniary interest in the matter in that they had subjected themselves to a *detriment* it was held that 'it does not matter whether the result of the vote would be to the pecuniary interest or disinterest of the person voting.' Interest in this sense can cover advantage or disadvantage.

The actual declaration of interest can be made by way of general notice to the proper officer of the authority or by particular notice when the occasion arises. General notices are recorded in a book which must be kept open to inspection by members of the authority.

A breach of the rule, whether by failing to disclose the interest, or by voting, or by taking part in the discussion prior to the vote, can lead to a fine not greater than £200, on summary conviction. It will be a defence to show that the member in question did not know that the matter in which he had an interest was being discussed.

It is the duty of the Director of Public Prosecutions to institute proceedings, but there is no rule stating who should bring the breach of the rules to his notice. It is suggested generally that the responsibility to inform the D.P.P. rests with the chairman of the council through the chief constable, through the latter has a discretion to withhold the facts from the D.P.P. if in his view the matter is *de minimis.*

Where an 'interested' person is barred from speaking or voting under the rule the Secretary of State (or the district council in the case of parish or community councils) can remove the disability, either completely, or in respect of speaking to the matter in question. Where an application for dispensation is proposed the member with the pecuniary interest can speak and vote on the matter.

In some cases a disabled person under the rule insists on speaking or voting. The chairman is then probably justified in refusing to count his vote. In *Nell v. Longbottom* (1894) a mayor-elect voted for himself and it was held his vote was invalid. Certainly, where a council is acting in a quasi-judicial capacity control may also be exercised by the courts on the principle of natural justice: in *R. v. Hendon Rural District Council* (1933) it was held that in such a case a vote cast by a member having an interest may make the decision void as offending the rule of natural justice on account of bias.

Claims for Allowances. By sections 173 to 178 of the Local Government Act 1972 payment of allowances may be made to members of local authorities and other bodies such as joint boards, joint committees, valuation panels and other prescribed bodies where the members are carrying out approved duties. These allowances are paid in respect of attendance, financial loss, travelling and subsistence.

While the council member has an entitlement to these allowances, co-opted members may claim financial loss allowances where they necessarily lose earnings or are put to additional expense because of their approved duties. Aldermen in the Greater London authorities may choose either, and thereafter must keep to their choice.

Travelling allowances are payable to members (other than parish and community council members) in respect of all approved duties inside or outside the authority's area and subject to no minimum distance. A subsistence allowance is payable where duty takes the member more than three miles from his home. For parish and community council members travelling expenses are payable only where the approved duty lies outside the parish, community or grouped parish or community, while subsistence allowances can be paid only where the duty lies outside the parish and is more than three miles from the member's home.

The expenses incurred in making official and courtesy visits may be defrayed by the local authority, inside or outside the United Kingdom, and those authorities which operate public service vehicles can give travel concessions to members for use in the performance of their approved duties.

But what is meant by 'approved duty'? Section 177 of the Local Government Act 1972 defines it as attendances at meetings and the doing of other things, or classes of things, for the purposes of the authority or body and approved by that authority or body (including service on or for other prescribed bodies to which the member is nominated or appointed by the council under a statutory power or duty).

The chairman, vice-chairman or deputy chairman of a principal council is not to be regarded as having a pecuniary interest in the allowance paid him so as to render him liable under the disclosure of interest provisions. Similarly, section 94 of the 1972 Act states that travelling, subsistence or attendance allowances to members do not cause those members to be regarded as having a pecuniary interest disabling them from voting.

Disqualification. By section 85 of the 1972 Act if a member fails for six months to attend a meeting of the authority or its committees, subcommittees, or joint committees or joint boards with which it is linked, he ceases to be a member, unless the authority has approved his absence during that period. The six-month period will run from the date of his last appearance at a meeting.

Section 92 of the Act also allows electors to challenge a person's right to act as a member, on the grounds that he is disqualified in law. The action may be brought in the High Court or in a court of summary jurisdiction, unless the person challenged has not acted, but simply claimed to be entitled to act – in this case, proceedings can be in the High Court only for a declaratory judgment, and if required an injunction.

Proceedings which show that the person challenged has acted while disqualified can result in his being fined up to £50 for each occasion on which he so acted. In a High Court hearing the office can be declared vacant and an injunction may be granted to prevent further acts on the part of the person challenged. In *Bishop v. Deakin* (1936) it was held that the limitation period for bringing such actions – which is six months – runs from the earliest date upon which the disqualified person acted. If magistrates dealing with a case consider it should more properly be dealt with in the High Court discontinuance of the proceedings may be ordered. A defendant in such an action may also apply to the High Court for an order to have the summary court's proceedings discontinued.

Officers

By section 112 of the Local Government Act 1972 an authority must appoint such officers as it thinks necessary for the proper discharge of its functions and the carrying out of its commitments on behalf of other authorities. Greater flexibility has been introduced into appointments by the Act for fewer *prescribed* officers need be appointed; some have still to be appointed, however, where committee members are appointed by persons or bodies other than the local authority. Thus, chief constables and their deputies and assistant chief constables must be appointed under the Police Act 1964, while National Park officers must be appointed under Schedule 17 of the 1972 Act. Additionally, section 112(4) lays down particular officers who must be appointed for specific purposes, namely:

(*a*) district surveyors and deputy district surveyors of the Greater London Council;[4]

(*b*) chief education officers;[5]

(*c*) chief officers and other members of fire brigades;[6]

(*d*) inspectors of weights and measures;[7]

(*e*) chief education officer of the Inner London Education Authority;[8]

(*f*) agricultural analysts and deputy agricultural analysts;[9]

(*g*) directors of social services.[10]

Furthermore, where the authority appoints a person for a specific function, such as a public analyst, it does not have the full discretion in appointment otherwise accepted by the Act. Apart from these cases, however, the authority may make such appointments as it deems necessary under section 112, and may appoint whoever it wishes to the posts. But there are exceptions to this principle.

(1) A member of an authority cannot be appointed by that authority to any paid office other than chairman or vice-chairman either while he remains a member, or for twelve months after membership ceases: section 116, Local Government Act 1972. In *Attorney-General v. Ulverston Urban District Council* (1944) it was held that even an honorary appointment was a 'paid office' in this respect.

(2) Where an authority wishes to appoint a director of social services it must send a list of persons from whom the selection is to be made to the Secretary of State for Social Services, who may prohibit the appointment of any person he regards as unsuitable: section 6, Local Authority Social Services Act 1970.

Conditions of Appointment. Officers appointed by the authorities are subject to the same statutory conditions and common-law provisions as other workers – so that, for instance, common-law duties of fidelity and proper performance apply as do statutory provisions such as the Contracts of Employment Act 1972. Equally, they can expect the authorities to undertake the responsibility, imposed by the Health and Safety at Work Act 1974, of ensuring so far as is reasonably practicable the health, safety and welfare at work of all the employees (see page 27) but certain groups are subject to special rules – the police and the fire services provide examples. Again, the fixing of wages by local authorities is now subject to collective-bargaining systems laid down by the Terms and Conditions of Employment Act 1959, and in practice the power of local authorities to exercise much discretion in such matters has been curtailed. In *Carr v. District Auditor for No. 1 Audit District* (1952) the district auditor accepted the recommendations of a joint negotiating committee as a basis for a measure of 'reasonableness' in exercising discretion over a salary payment; the court held he was wrong, for his question should have been: Was the salary paid by the council objectively unreasonable?

It is certain that officers cannot legally receive gratuities from the authority: though it was said in *Re Magrath* (1934) that the case might be different where 'the officer or servant was asked to perform extra services in respect of a specified job or undertaking, on the understanding that as soon as the work was complete the authority would determine the amount of his special remuneration'.

The Local Government Act 1972 also deals with pecuniary interests. By section 117, if an officer learns that a contract in which he has a direct or indirect pecuniary interest (other than one to which he himself is a party) has been, or is proposed to be concluded by the authority, he must disclose his interest in writing. Section 115 forbids him, in addition, under his office or employment to exact or accept any fee or reward other than is proper remuneration. A breach of sections 115 or 117 can lead to summary conviction and a fine not exceeding £200.

His common-law duty to account for money and property committed to his charge for his employer is supplemented by section 115, and section 114 places a duty upon the authority to take security with respect to officers who are likely to have control of money; it may also take security for other officers, and other persons who are not employed by the authority but who may nevertheless have control of money or property.

The general responsibilities of officers employed by local authorities lie towards the employing authority and towards the general public. Legally, the officers are the servants of the council which appoints them and though they may give advice as experts to the elected members they must act under the orders of the council and its committees. In some cases officers are given discretionary powers to act in their own behalf – the medical officer of health obviously will be called upon to exercise a certain professional skill. On the other hand, where a treasurer is ordered to make a payment which is illegal he cannot use 'discretion' in the matter, nor, if he makes the payment, can he plead that he was merely obeying the orders of the employing authority. He would be personally liable. In *Attorney-General v. De Winton* (1906) it was said: 'the treasurer is not a mere servant of the council: he owes a duty and stands in a fiduciary relation to the burgesses as a body . . . and although he holds office during the pleasure of the council only this does not enable him to plead the orders of the council as an excuse for an unlawful act'. Similarly, the position of the town clerk was discussed in *Re Hurle-Hobbs* (1944) as follows:

> The office of town clerk is an important part of the machinery of local government. He may be said to stand between the borough council and the ratepayers. He is there to assist by his advice and

action the conduct of public affairs in the borough, and if there is a disposition on the part of the council, still more on the part of any member of the council, to ride roughshod over his opinions, the questions must at once arise as to whether or not it is his duty forthwith to resign his office or, at any rate, to do what he thinks right and await the consequences.

This does not mean that officers employed by the authorities should disregard orders given to them and act as they see fit – they are not independent. Nevertheless, where the orders are clearly unlawful it is well to remember that the shield of incorporation can be lifted, and the individual officer who has disregarded a lawful order, or carried out an unlawful one, may find himself personally liable.

Nor should the officer's duty towards members of the public be forgotten. The borough surveyor may give opinions as may the architect and engineer, on matters affecting building and construction, slum-clearance, demolition, road-widening and traffic schemes. The opinion may be given as an answer to an enquiry from a member of the public. In such cases, there are two matters of concern. First, the officer giving the opinion must display a proper professional standard in his action or statement, and, second, he may hold a duty of care towards the person making the enquiry which is based not on a contractual situation between them, but a tortious one. Thus, the architect who gives wrong information may be sued in negligence, as may other officers in similar situations. Before 1964 the situation was that liability followed only if physical loss or damage was shown, but the important case of *Hedley Byrne & Co. Ltd v. Heller & Partners Ltd* (1964) established that a negligent misstatement, even though made honestly, may give rise to an action for damages for financial loss caused as a result of the statement, since the law implies a duty of care where

(a) the party seeking information from a person having a special skill (such as an architect) expects him to exercise due care; and

(b) the person possessing the special skill knew or should have known his skill and judgment were being relied upon.

A case in point arose in *Dutton v. Bognor Regis Urban District Council* (1972). A developer applied to the local authority for permission to build; this was given subject to the authority's surveyor examining the foundations. The local authority's inspector was negligent in his inspection, the house was completed, and when defects appeared in it the plaintiff sued the authority for the cost of repairs and the fall in market value of the house. The Court of Appeal held that but for the inspector's error the house would have been built upon secure foundations so the authority was liable for the act of its employee – the inspector. The local authority was by statute and its own by-laws invested with control over building operations and any negligence in the exercise of that power of control would, if damage resulted, be enough to ground an action. Similar situations have arisen in the case of negligent replies to local land charges searches[11] and to enquiries.[12]

It is noteworthy, however, that the person making the statement can effectively avoid liability, simply by stating clearly to the enquirer that he accepts no responsibility for the accuracy of his statement. Equally, if he makes the caveat that he has given the statement without taking the time for consideration or further enquiry which a careful answer would require, he can escape liability under the negligent misstatement rule.

Medical officers of health and public health inspectors had, in the past, been given power under the Public Health Act 1961 to act on behalf of the authority employing them; similarly, local planning authorities could delegate some of their powers to officers who could take decisions on behalf of the authorities.[13] But these positions were exceptional, even though in practical terms officers generally took decisions and actions within their general authority which were regarded as the acts of the council.

The exceptional situation was made regular by the Local Government Act 1972 which gave a general power to local authorities to discharge *any* of their functions through officers. While the position is thus regularised, it still remains open to question how far an officer can bind his authority by acts he carries out which are not *strictly* within the bounds of the formal delegation by the employing authority.

It is certainly clear that formal delegation is necessary where a power of decision is given to a local authority by statute: if the officer acts without such formal delegation he does not bind the authority. In *Princes Investment Ltd v. Frimley and Camberley Urban District Council* (1962) the engineer who gave approval to the layout of the company's sewers had not been given the power to do so by resolution of the council so his approval was not binding on the authority. It was argued for the company that approvals fell within the normal day-to-day business transacted by the engineer and no resolution should therefore be necessary but the court rejected this view.

It is also clear that the authority is not bound by an officer's acts where the acts effectively hinder or prevent the authority from exercising a discretion conferred upon it by statute. In *Southend-on-Sea*

Corporation v. Hodgson (Wickford) Ltd (1962) a builder relied upon the borough engineer's statement that planning consent for certain land was not necessary. When the authority later said it *was* necessary the builder argued that the authority was estopped from saying so, but the court held that estoppel (that is, the rule which prevents a party from denying the truth of a statement previously made by him, or the existence of facts which by words or conduct he has led other persons to believe in) could not be used to hinder the exercise of a statutory discretion vested in a public authority. This principle must nevertheless be looked at against the background of the general rule of 'ostensible authority' – that is, the authority which ostensibly is given to a person exercising a particular function. When an authority employs an architect he will possess, ostensibly, all that authority which architects in similar situations normally possess. Where he, or an engineer, or a surveyor, or a planning officer, or any other officer, acts within the scope of his ostensible authority and makes a representation upon which some other persons act the employing authority will be bound by it, in the same way that a private person or a commercial company would be bound. As Lord Denning M.R. said: 'If the planning officer tells the developer that a proposed variation is not material, and the developer acts upon it, the planning authority cannot go back on it. I know that there are authorities which say that a public authority cannot be estopped by any representations made by its officers. It cannot be estopped from doing its public duty . . . But these statements must now be taken with considerable reserve.'[14] In *Norfolk County Council v. Secretary of State for the Environment* (1973), where an officer mistakenly sent out a planning consent the Lord Chief Justice firmly based his judgment on the principle of estoppel.

Committees

Much of the work of the local authorities is carried out through committees. Their membership is fixed by the council and with the exception of finance committees they may include co-opted members – up to one-third of the total membership. The Local Government Act 1972 lists, in section 101(9), a number of statutory committees where the composition is dealt with by statute – for instance, social services, police and education committees. No member can be forced to serve on a particular committee; a council can remove a member even though he is duly appointed for the ensuing year.

The 1972 Act gives an authority a general power to arrange for a committee or subcommittee to discharge any of its functions. Some decisions will be subject to confirmation by the council, however, but others will become effective as soon as they are made by the committee or subcommittee.

Where a decision needs confirmation by the authority, confirmation makes the decision in all respects a decision of the council, so that where, as in *Goddard v. Minister of Housing and Local Government* (1958), it was argued that the *council itself* had not looked into the issue in question but had merely 'rubber-stamped' the committee decision, the court held the decision was effective, for the council had acted through its committee. Similarly, action taken before confirmation might be beyond the delegated power of the committee, but subsequent confirmation would amount to a ratification of the act, as in *Firth v. Staines* (1897).

Though an authority might have specifically delegated to a committee the power to make decisions on certain matters it does not mean the council cannot exercise the relevant function itself. It can withdraw the delegated power at any time, or even exercise the power itself without withdrawal (subject to any third party rights that might have arisen). Moreover, although the general principle is *delegatus non potest delegare* (a person to whom powers are delegated cannot delegate them to another), this does not apply where an authority delegates a power to a committee, for, unless it otherwise directs, that power can be delegated by the committee to a subcommittee or to an officer.

One power which cannot be delegated to a committee or subcommittee is the power to levy a rate or issue a precept or borrow money – this power can be exercised only by the authority itself.

By section 102 of the 1972 Act authorities can discharge their functions through joint committees and, while there is no general power to create joint boards, section 241 of the 1972 Act contains a power enabling the provisions of the Act to be extended to joint boards.

Meetings

The rules governing the meetings of local authorities and of their committees are set out in Schedule 12 to the Local Government Act 1972 but authorities may make, in addition, standing orders to regulate proceedings and the despatch of business. It should be added that rules of the common law relating to meetings will also apply.

Under the rules laid down in Schedule 12 a principal council will hold an annual meeting and such other meetings as the council deems necessary. The quorum is one-quarter of the council and the chairman will, normally, preside. Similar rules apply in respect of parish councils and community councils except that the annual meeting is obligatory and at least three other meetings must be held each year, and they must not be held in licensed premises unless there is no other suitable accommodation. Parish meetings are required to meet annually between 1 March and 1 June and matters discussed may be decided upon by a simple majority of those present and voting. Since community meetings are not continuing bodies with executive functions there is no requirement as to regular meetings.

As far as committee meetings are concerned, section 106 of the Local Government Act 1972 confers upon local authorities a general power to make standing orders with regard to the quorum, proceedings and place of meetings of committees and joint committees, and, subject to standing orders, these are determined by the committee itself. Normally, the majority present and voting will carry the day, but if there is no majority the person presiding will have a casting vote. The minutes are kept in a minute-book and are signed at the same or following meeting. The minutes must be kept open for inspection.

Apart from these general provisions, normally found in standing orders, an important area of law has grown up in relation to meetings in the law relating to defamation. A defamatory statement has been defined as one which exposes a person to hatred, ridicule or contempt, or which causes him to be shunned or avoided, or which has a tendency to injure him in his profession, trade or calling. The person who utters such a statement commits the tort of defamation: if it is in permanent form, such as writing, it is libel; if it is in transient form, such as the word, slander. The person committing the tort is then liable for the consequences which flow from his act, and may be sued for damages. Not only persons in the individual sense can bring such an action; in *Bognor Regis Urban District Council v. Campion* (1972) it was held that a council can successfully bring an action against a ratepayer who publishes leaflets defamatory of the council.

Liability in defamation is strict; statute apart, it need not be shown that the defendant either intended to defame or could have avoided it by the exercise of reasonable care. Nevertheless, certain defences are available, most notably the defence of 'privilege'. There are two kinds of privilege – absolute and qualified. Absolute privilege attaches to a limited range of proceedings, mainly judicial and parliamentary and is a complete answer to any charge of defamation. The basis of qualified privilege is the need for people to communicate with each other in good faith regarding certain matters without fear of having to substantiate the truth of what they say in a court of law. It is recognised that such situations exist – in particular, where the person uttering the statement has an interest or a duty, which is legal, social or moral, in making it to another, who has a corresponding duty or interest in receiving it.

The defence of qualified privilege is 'qualified' in the sense that the existence of malice will destroy it as a defence. It is an important defence for council and committee meetings, however, and under the Public Bodies (Admission to Meetings) Act 1960 qualified privilege applies to agenda and certain other documents supplied to the Press, or the public attending the meeting, and relating to matters that lie before the local authority and other bodies.

In addition, other defences to a claim in defamation are possible. Truth, or justification, provides one defence; equally, it is a good defence to show that the statement was made as a fair comment upon a matter of public interest, honestly believed to be true, and not inspired by malice. It must also be shown that the statements of fact on which the comment was based were *materially* (not necessarily completely) true. Thus, if the *purpose* of the communication is improper, such as ulterior motive or gaining some financial advantage, the defence is lost.

Further defences are available to newspapers: under section 2 of the Libel Act 1843 it is a defence to show that the statement was published without actual malice or negligence, and the earliest opportunity was taken to publish an apology. Payment into court by way of amends must also be made. The Defamation Act 1952 extended the general principle: by section 7, fair and accurate reports of meetings of local authorities and their committees are privileged provided they were not actuated by malice. It should be noted that this qualified privilege does not extend to meetings to which the public and the Press are denied entry and to use the defence the newspaper must show that a reasonable letter was published by way of contradiction or explanation (if this was requested).

POWERS OF LOCAL AUTHORITIES

Some of the more important powers of local authorities are dealt with in Chapters 3 to 8 of this book but it may be noted here that all such powers are derived from statutory provisions. Most local authority

powers are obtained by public Acts of Parliament, but there are two
other ways in which powers can be acquired.

First, it is possible for a local authority to obtain powers by means of a
local Act, which will be specific to that authority and go beyond those
powers conferred by the public Act.

Second, an authority may take up those powers which are generally
available but which cannot be obtained without some special steps being
taken, such as provisional order procedure or special parliamentary
procedure.

The general public Acts which confer specific powers on authorities
are dealt with later: we may here look at the other sources, including
adoptive Acts.

Local Acts of Parliament

After due public notice and the presentation of a petition for leave to
introduce the Bill in Parliament, a Bill may be introduced to pass
through the usual stages of first reading and second reading and then
go before a committee for the committee stage. Counsel who practise at
the Parliamentary Bar here plead the cases for the promoters and the
objectors to the Bill, with individual clauses being contested and reports
of government departments considered. Thereafter, the successful Bill
obtains its third reading and goes to the House of Lords to pass through
similar stages before obtaining the Royal Assent.

The local Act of Parliament effectively has the same status as a public
Act in that the courts of law cannot question its validity. The argument
was recently raised that a court was competent to go behind a *private* Act
of Parliament to investigate the circumstances, where it was claimed
that the Act had been improperly obtained by misleading Parliament,
but the House of Lords in *British Railways Board v. Pickin* (1973) held
that a court of law can go behind no Act of Parliament, public or
private.

The power of construing Acts of Parliament is one that does remain
to the courts of law and in this matter the courts construe private Acts
strictly against the authority or person promoting them and liberally in
favour of the public, on the ground that 'persons who obtain a private
Act ought to take care that it is so worded that that which they desire to
obtain for themselves is plainly stated' and the public interest must be
protected against the strictly 'parochial' interest sought to be covered by
the private Act. The number of private Acts of Parliament that have
been obtained is large, many of them going back into the early

nineteenth century, so although the Local Government Act 1972 specifically provided that local legislation in force on 1 April 1974 should remain in force, section 262 also stipulated that the Secretary of State, or an appropriate Minister, may by order extend it to the whole of the new local government area, but at the end of 1979 such local Acts shall cease to be effective.[15] Local provisions may be exempted from this repeal by the Secretary of State or other appropriate Minister, and the date itself may be postponed.

Provisional Order Procedure

The promotion of local Bills has always been an expensive process and provisional order procedure was introduced as a method of cutting down such expense. Section 240 of the Local Government Act 1972 now states that the procedure to be followed in the making of a provisional order under the Act, or under any enactment passed on or after 1 June 1934 is:

(1) the applicants must publicise the order;
(2) objections are considered by the Secretary of State;
(3) a local enquiry is held unless the Secretary of State considers this unnecessary;
(4) the Secretary of State makes a provisional order and submits it for confirmation to Parliament;
(5) if a petitioner presents a petition against the pending confirmation he may appear before the Select Committee which has taken reference of the provisional order, and may oppose it as if it were a private Bill.

The procedure which applies to provisional orders under statutes enacted before 1 June 1934 is stated in those statutes.

Orders Subject to Special Parliamentary Procedure

The Statutory Orders (Special Procedure) Act 1945, as amended by the 1965 Act of the same name and section 240 of the Local Government Act 1972, lays down a more straightforward method of acquiring powers. The first step is the making of an order by the Minister; notice is given in the *London Gazette* and in at least one local newspaper in the area, and then the order is laid before Parliament.

Petitions against the order can be laid within 21 days. Objections may have been heard before lodgement and a local enquiry may have been held, but once the order lies before Parliament it is still possible to make petitions of general objection, as well as petitions for amendment which are related to specific and particular amendments. A report is made to the House[16] and within 21 days of the report the House may annul the order. If no annulment is made the order can come into operation at the end of the resolution period, provided no petition for amendment has been made. If such a petition has been presented the order will stand referred to a Joint Committee of both Houses, whereas if there has been a petition of general objection it will stand referred to the Joint Committee unless either House resolves otherwise. The Joint Committee may report the order with or without amendment – in the latter case the order becomes operative from the day the report is laid before Parliament. If the order contains an amendment it becomes effective, duly amended, on a day fixed by the Minister (unless he withdraws it or resubmits it to the House for further consideration by way of a Confirmation Bill).

Adoptive Acts

In practice much of the legislative activity of local authorities is undertaken by use of the adoptive Acts procedure whereby local authorities formally adopt statutory provisions which are public and general in nature. The Local Government Act 1972 extended the adoptive provisions contained in the Public Health Acts 1875 to 1925[17] to all England and Wales, whether adopted or not, but there are still a number of Acts that contain adoptive provisions which do not take effect in any local authority area unless formally adopted by that authority. Thus, the advance payments code (see page 93) can be adopted, under the Highways Act 1959 in parishes and communities by resolution of the county council, and a licensing system can be adopted by a local authority under the adoptive provisions of the Private Places of Entertainment (Licensing) Act 1967.

Originating Legislation

Although local authorities tend to use the procedures noted above for the acquisition of most of their powers it should not be assumed that they never originate legislation – indeed, over the years the authorities have promoted many private Bills to obtain powers they would not otherwise obtain. Some of these Acts have been 'adopted' by other authorities, who have written their provisions into their own private Bills, with some clauses receiving the accolade of transposition into general legislation. Nor should the influence of the local authority associations be discounted, since they actively consider existing legislation and both formally and informally bring influence to bear upon the government departments responsible for the drafting of legislative measures.

THE DUTIES OF LOCAL AUTHORITIES

A distinction must be drawn between the powers and the duties of local authorities. There are many statutory provisions which give local authorities the power to do certain things; there are others which impose positive duties upon the authorities – by which the authority is placed under a legal obligation to act.

The question of controls exercised over the powers and administrative discretions of local authorities can be left to the next chapter, but we may here deal with the enforcement of those public duties that are imposed upon the local authorities.

It is necessary first to distinguish between those statutes which create powers and those which create duties. It is clear that where an authority is placed under an absolute duty in law to carry out a certain function the situation is straightforward but the position is not always so clear-cut. A case in point arose in *Dutton v. Bognor Regis Urban District Council* (1972)[18] where Lord Denning M.R. said:[19]

> Much discussion took place before us as to whether the council were under a *duty* to examine the foundations or had only a *power* to do so. The Public Health Acts do not make this clear. The Act of 1936 simply says that it is the duty of the local authority to carry the Act into execution: see section 1(1). The Act of 1961 says that it is the function of every local authority to enforce building regulations in their district. The word 'function' may mean either a power or a duty.
>
> The reason for this discussion was the case of *East Suffolk Rivers Catchment Board v. Kent.*[20] The argument was that if the local authority had a mere *power* to examine the foundations, they were not liable for not exercising that power. But if they were under a *duty* to do so, they would be liable for not doing it. This argument assumes that the functions of a local authority can be divided into two categories, powers and duties. Every function must be put into one or the other category. It is either a *power* or a *duty*. This is, however, a mistake. There is a middle term. It is *control.*
>
> In this case, the significant thing, to my mind, is that the legislature gives the local authority a great deal of *control* over building work and the way it is done. . . .

In my opinion, the control thus entrusted to the local authority is so extensive that it carries with it a duty.

The position is further confused in that, in spite of Lord Denning's words, the court actually found on the basis of negligence by the surveyor, rather than on the council's failure to exercise its powers. A further word of warning should be added. Many statutes use the word 'duty' without actually placing a legally enforceable obligation upon the authority, because of the fact that the 'duty' is so loosely phrased as to be virtually unenforceable. An example is seen in the National Health Service Act 1946: 'It shall be the duty of the Minister of Health . . . to promote the establishment in England and Wales of a comprehensive health service . . .' It is obvious that the duty so imposed is one that would need political rather than legal enforcement.

The first stage, then, is to determine whether a power or a duty exists. The next step is to discover whether the statute in question provides a remedy for the injury complained of. The general principle is that where a statute provides penalties there is *prima facie* no civil remedy, for if this were not so crimes would too easily be turned into torts. It is true that actions are sometimes allowed in such cases, particularly under the Factories Act, but in general such actions are not possible. Thus, the remedy provided by section 72 of the Public Health Act 1936 (by which the occupier who has served notice on the authority of its failure to take away house rubbish can claim 25p for each day while the default continues) would preclude an action in damages; equally, damages could not be claimed where the Act provides arbitration and assessment of compensation. In all cases, however, it is the *whole* Act which is looked at.

But what if a duty is imposed and no special remedy or penalty is prescribed? The situation then is that the courts will decide whether the duty to provide the service in question is one that is owed to the community at large, or to individuals, of whom the complainant is one. Only in the latter case will the individual be able to claim damages. In other words, the individual must show he is an 'aggrieved party' within the terms of the Act. According to Veale J. in *Reffell v. Surrey County Council* (1964) the questions to be asked by the court are:

(1) Was the action brought in respect of the kind of harm which the statute was intended to prevent?

(2) Was the person bringing the action one of the class which the statute desired to protect?

(3) Was the special remedy provided by the statute adequate for the protection of the person injured?

If the answers to (1) and (2) are affirmative and to (3) negative, an action will lie and damages can be won.

Many such actions are brought in negligence where the complainant argues that the authority's failure to exercise its functions amount to negligence and an action then lies in respect of the resulting damage, loss or injury. An action is also possible in the tort of nuisance, however, where the plaintiff can show that there has been an act or omission which amounts to an interference with, disturbance of, or annoyance to the exercise of his ownership or occupation of land, or of other right used or enjoyed in connection with land. The possibility is important for, as was pointed out in *Pride of Derby and Derbyshire Angling Association v. British Celanese* (1953), non-feasance, in the sense of failure to perform some positive statutory duty, did not give rise to an action in negligence against the local authority in respect of its sewerage system: it was necessary to show misfeasance. In an action based on nuisance, on the other hand, the distinction between non-feasance and misfeasance is irrelevant. The warning should be added that this case cannot be regarded as authority for the principle in general, however, for the decision was based on an element of misfeasance – the discharge of insufficiently treated sewage into the river. On the question of liability in negligence the leading case must now be regarded as *Dutton v. Bognor Regis Urban District Council* (1972).

The court held in that case that the negligent approval of the foundations of the house (which had been built on a rubbish tip) amounted to a breach of the authority's duty. It also held that the purchaser of the house was within the 'neighbour principle' as being a person so closely and directly affected by the inspector's act that he ought to have her in mind as likely to be injured when he made his inspection. That liability of the council extended to economic loss as well as physical injury and while the authority contended that the claim amounted to an application of negligence to a new situation, Lord Denning M.R. countered by saying:

What are the considerations of policy here? . . . First, Mrs Dutton has suffered a grievous loss. The house fell down without any fault of hers. She is in no position herself to bear the loss. Who ought in justice to bear it? I should think those who are responsible. Who are they? In the first place the builder was responsible. It was he who laid the foundations so badly that the house fell down. In the second place, the council's inspector was responsible. It was his job to examine the foundations to see if they would take the load of the house. He failed to do it properly. In the third place, the council should answer for his failure. They were entrusted by Parliament with the task of seeing that houses were properly built. They received public funds for the purpose. The very object was to protect purchasers and occupiers of houses. Yet they failed to protect them. Their shoulders are broad enough to bear the loss.

Lord Denning also discussed the argument that the inspector employed by the council owed no duty to the purchaser. He said that since *Hedley Byrne & Co. Ltd v. Heller & Partners Ltd* (1964) it was clear that where a professional man gives guidance to others he owes a duty of care not only to his client who employs him but also to others who he knows are relying on his special skill to save them from the likelihood of injury. In the situation where a professional man gives advice on the safety of buildings or machines or materials or methods of construction his duty lies to all who may be injured if his advice is bad.

General Duties

The powers and duties placed upon local authorities with regard to the discharge of functions are discussed elsewhere in this book (p. 19), but there are some duties placed on local authorities which are of general application. Two such duties may be looked at by way of examples – the duty an authority might owe as an occupier of premises, and the duty an authority might owe as an employer.

Occupiers Liability Act 1957.

There are certain common-law rules which regulate in part the duty an occupier owes to the public with regard to premises, but here we may look specifically at the statutory liability placed upon all occupiers, including local authorities.

Section 2 of the Act states that an occupier owes a common duty of care to all visitors to his premises, except in so far as he extends, modifies, restricts or excludes his duty to any visitor(s) by agreement or otherwise. The common duty of care is a duty 'to take such care as in all the circumstances of the case is reasonable to see that the visitor will be reasonably safe in using the premises for the purposes for which he is invited or permitted by the occupier to be there'.

Section 2(3) lays down circumstances which would be looked at as relevant to ascertaining the degree of care or want of care. It states that occupiers must be prepared for children to be less careful than adults, but can expect a person 'in the exercise of his calling' to guard against special risks ordinarily arising in his work. Subsection (4) points out that a warning *in itself* will not absolve the occupier of liability to the visitor (though it may play a part in deciding whether the occupier has been negligent) and adds that if the occupier has acted reasonably in entrusting construction, maintenance or repair work to an independent contractor he will not be liable for faulty work done, provided he took reasonable steps to check on the competence of the contractor.

A visitor who willingly accepts risks on entering premises will not be able to make a claim for injuries from the occupier, and there is no duty of care towards a trespasser. In *British Railways Board v. Herrington* (1971) a child strayed through a broken fence on to an electrified line and was injured. The stationmaster knew children strayed there and knew also the fence had not been repaired. The board was held to be liable to the six-year-old child injured, in spite of the trespasser rule, because of the special circumstances involving the proximity of the line to the public pathway and the likelihood of grave danger for a child who would be unaware of that danger. In all cases of this nature, therefore, the particular circumstances are of importance.

The position has particular application for a corporation in *Harris v. Birkenhead Corporation* (1974). The corporation served on the house-owner in a clearance area a notice to treat and notice of entry under the 1957 Housing Act. The tenant left before Christmas, after telling the corporation. Vandals then damaged the premises, which became derelict and an infant trespasser fell from the second-floor window and was injured. Was the corporation liable to the infant trespasser? The court held that when the house was vacated the corporation became, effectively, the occupiers; they must have had notice of the condition of the house and should thus have anticipated the danger; and a derelict house with a gaping window only a few inches above the floor and openly available to a four-year-old child was a potentially dangerous situation against which any humane and common-sense person ought to take the precautions. The corporation were, therefore, liable.

Health and Safety at Work Act 1974. The Robens Report on Safety and Health at Work felt that 150 years of legislation had created too much unintelligible law and the result was the passing of a new Act in 1974 which substantially repeated, in section 2, the common-law precepts on safety. Under the Act every employer has a duty to ensure, so far as is reasonably practicable, the health, safety and welfare at work of all his employees. Examples are stated in the Act, including the provision of plant and systems of work and their maintenance; the use, handling, storage and transport of articles and substances; the provision of instruction, training and supervision; the provision and maintenance of a proper working environment.

The Factories Act, the Mines and Quarries Act and similar legislation presently remains in force but will be repealed in due course. By and large the new Act leans heavily on the experience obtained in the working of these Acts. But it also introduces new liabilities for some – in particular, the designers, manufacturers, importers, suppliers, installers, erectors of articles and substances for use at work. After 1 April 1975 they must take 'reasonably practicable' steps to ensure the safety of their goods and equipment in their ultimate industrial use (section 6).

The general duties under the Act are not of the same strict variety as is seen under the Factories Act, so particular circumstances are of importance. And the employee must take reasonable care for the safety and health of himself and of others who might be affected by his acts, or by his failure to act.

The furtherance of the general purposes of the Act is placed in the hands of the Health and Safety Commission and the Health and Safety Executive; the Commission is empowered to make and issue codes of practice, and the responsibility for inspection is under the Act to be reviewed by the Secretary of State, for possible reallocation between existing Inspectorate services, local authorities included, so as to remove 'any uncertainty as to ... respective responsibility for the enforcement of provisions'.

THE DOCTRINE OF ULTRA VIRES

Powers of administration are creatures of statute. A statute gives power for specified purposes, or subjects the use of the power to some special procedure, or places some other kind of limitation upon its use. Such limits are to be found in the rules of construction which the courts have applied over the years, and it follows that any act by an authority which is outside the prescribed limits amounts to an abuse of power by the authority. It is acting *ultra vires*, outside its powers.

The rigid application of the doctrine of *ultra vires*, by which any act outside the conferred powers would be void, would lead to an impossible situation and as long ago as 1880 the courts stated that corporations could do not only those things for which they had an express or implied authority, but also whatever was reasonably incidental to the doing of those things. Section 111 of the Local Government Act 1972 gave the common-law rule statutory effect by empowering authorities to do anything which is calculated to facilitate, or is conducive to or incidental to the discharge of any of their functions.

Nevertheless, the doctrine still has important application in that the questions can still be asked of the exercise of any particular function:

(1) Is the act specifically authorised by statute?
(2) If not, can authority be reasonably implied from the wording of the statute?
(3) If not, and if there is no direct or implied authority, is the act reasonably incidental to the carrying out of a statutory function?

Breach of the Rule

Where an authority has acted *ultra vires* a High Court action may be commenced – a ratepayer, for instance, may ask for a declaration, or a declaration coupled with an injunction in the High Court (see page 39). In *Smith v. Cardiff Corporation* (1955) the application – by council-house tenants for a declaration that a differential rent scheme was *ultra vires* – was unsuccessful; in *Prescott v. Birmingham Corporation* (1955) the ratepayers succeeded in obtaining a declaration that the granting of free bus travel to old-age pensioners was *ultra vires*. But High Court actions are expensive and usually such actions must be commenced in conjunction with the Attorney-General (the *relator* action). The Attorney-General's standing-in at the instance of the plaintiff can be useful where the plaintiff might have difficulty otherwise in showing that he has any *locus standi* in the eyes of the court, but it does make for another hurdle to be surmounted. In *Prescott's* case (above) it was held, however, that the court may grant a declaration to a ratepayer without any objection of *locus standi*, although the decision is far from clear since Mr Prescott's 'standing' was not discussed by the court.

The *ultra vires* breach may also be discovered and acted upon by a district auditor, who may apply to the court for a declaration to that effect, unless the expenditure in question has been authorised by the Secretary of State. Members or officers who are held responsible for the *ultra vires* expenditure can be called upon to account for it through the statutory audit.

The likelihood of *ultra vires* actions arising has receded somewhat in recent years as a result of the Parliamentary practice of drawing powers widely when granting them to local authorities. Thus, section 137 of the Local Government Act 1972 gives a wide discretion to the authorities, who may spend up to the product of a 2p rate for the benefit of the area or a part of it or for the benefit of all or some of the inhabitants. Similar widely drawn provisions appear in sections 138 and 139. Again, by sections 120 and 124 authorities are empowered to buy land 'for the benefit, improvement or development of their areas'.

This is not to deny the existence of the doctrine, however, nor its importance. Its application may be made less fierce than in days gone by, but it still remains as one of the controlling influences upon the activities of local authorities.

It is, of course, not the only controlling influence. Essentially, it is part of the judicial control exercised over administrative bodies, and in the course of the next chapter we may look more broadly at the whole question of control, and at the more recent developments which have been superimposed upon long-established principles.

REFERENCES

1. English counties, metropolitan districts, London boroughs and the boundaries between Greater London and its adjoining counties and between the City of London and adjacent London boroughs: section 48.
2. In the case of authorities for the purposes of the Local Authorities Social Services Act 1970.
3. In the case of county councils.
4. Under ss. 75 or 80 London Building Acts 1939.
5. Section 88 of the Education Act 1944.
6. Those maintained under the Fire Services Act 1947.
7. Under section 41 of the Weights and Measures Act 1963.
8. Section 30(4) of the London Government Act 1963.
9. Section 67(3) of the Agriculture Act 1970.
10. Section 6 of the Local Authority Social Services Act 1970.
11. *Ministry of Housing v. Sharp* (1970).
12. *Coats Paton v. Birmingham Corporation* (1971).
13. By virtue of section 64, Town and Country Planning Act 1968.
14. *Lever (Finance) Ltd v. Westminster Corporation,* [1970] 3 W.L.R., p. 738.
15. In metropolitan counties. The end of 1984 elsewhere in England and Wales, outside the Greater London area.
16. By the Chairman of Ways and Means in the Commons; by the Lord Chairman of Committees in the Lords.
17. With certain exceptions.
18. The facts of this case are discussed on p. 25.

19. See [1972] 1 Q.B., pp. 391, 392.

20. The board in this case was sued for damages arising out of its failure to carry out repair works to river banks within a reasonable time. There was no statutory duty to repair – merely a power. It was held that the board could not be made liable in damages; so long as they acted honestly in the exercise of their discretion 'it is for them to determine the method by which and the time within which the power shall be exercised . . .'. [1941] A.C. 74, p. 102.

2

Control of Local Authorities

Apart from the general power of Parliament to grant and withdraw functions from local authorities – which is in itself a form of control – local authorities are often made subject to the formal control of Ministers and Departments of State in respect of some functions. Such formal controls – examples of which are seen in Education and the provision of Social Services – must stem from a specific statutory provision. They can also arise through a process of consultation and the issue of circulars to the local authorities. An example of this practice arose in the building licensing work undertaken by local authorities between 1945 and 1954 on behalf of the Ministry of Works. In addition to this there are other subtle forms of control – departmental advice, practice codes, circulars explaining a Minister's policy. A memorandum issued by the Department will not be binding upon a local authority, but it can well influence its decision. In the first instance, however, we may look at the forms of control that are laid down by Acts of Parliament.

STATUTORY FORMS OF CONTROL

Control over Borrowing

By the Local Government Act 1972 a local authority may borrow money for any purposes or class of purpose subject to the consent, approval and conditions laid down by the Secretary of State. The purpose must, however, be *intra vires* the authority. Circulars 2/70 and 66/71 of the Department of the Environment have lessened the extent to which this control can be exercised by the Secretary of State, since they give a general sanction to borrow for capital expenditure in 'key sector schemes', the acquisition of land for certain purposes including Part V of the Housing Act 1957, improvements under Parts I and II of the

Housing Act 1969, and locally determined schemes. The procedure is dealt with in more detail on page 155.

Grants

A form of control exists through the grant system. Generally, no specific grant will be payable unless a Minister is satisfied with the service for which the grant is claimed and usually the expenditure must be 'approved' expenditure. Though such grants are rarely withheld the threat remains and is essentially a control. An example appeared in the Housing Finance Act 1972. By section 6 subsidies were payable 'at such times and in such manner as the Treasury may direct, and subject to such conditions as to records, certificates, audit or otherwise as the Secretary of State may, with the approval of the Treasury, impose'. In the event of a default and the service of a default order by the Secretary of State, the housing subsidy could be reduced, suspended or discontinued.

The effect was that the Secretary of State was able to control the standards of local authority housing schemes. It was a discretionary power on his part: there was no appeal to Parliament or the courts.

Regulations

Statutes often confer powers on local authorities and at the same time authorise a Minister to make regulations as to how the work should be done and what standards should be reached or conditions fulfilled before a grant will be payable. This may seem to give Ministers unwarranted powers, but it does also give flexibility, for it is easier to change regulations than it is to change Acts of Parliament. Thus, in the Town and Country Planning Act 1971, sections 18 (submission and approval of local plans) and 24 (general development orders) give the Secretary of State power to limit and control the discretionary powers of local planning authorities in granting or withholding planning permission. The Town and Country Planning General Development Order 1973 was made under section 24 of the 1971 Act and provides an example of the Secretary of State's use of his powers of control.

It is noteworthy that such rules must be laid before Parliament, who can annul them in either House, but in practice Parliament rarely challenges such regulations in this way, being content to leave the power of control in the Secretary of State.

Inspection

Control by inspection arises mainly in the education, fire and police services. Thus, section 24 of the Fire Services Act 1947 enables the Crown and the Secretary of State to appoint inspectors who will in practice advise and encourage the acceptance of improved systems and techniques.

Defaulting Authorities

By section 17 of the Town and Country Planning Act 1971, where a local enquiry has been held and the Secretary of State for the Environment is satisfied that a planning authority has failed to carry out its functions regarding the preparation and submission of a structure or local plan, he may either take the functions over himself or transfer them to another planning authority with an interest in the proper planning of the area. This is an example of Parliament giving the Minister a specific power of control in the event of an authority defaulting in its statutory functions. The cost of carrying out the remedial work will fall upon the defaulting authority.

Scheme Approvals

Some statutes give local authorities a duty to prepare schemes, proposals or plans which must be submitted to the Minister concerned, showing him how they propose carrying out the obligations placed upon them by the Act. The Minister may then approve or reject the submission, or amend it. Once approved, the scheme is binding upon the authority. Examples are found in sections 6 and 7 of the Town and Country Planning Act 1971 (survey and structure plans for land development) and section 11 of the Education Act 1944 (development plan for the provision of schools in the area).

Effectively, in such cases, although the powers granted by the Acts to the local authorities are extremely wide they are thus made subject to close control by a Minister, since the structure plan is of primary importance in carrying out the planning powers, and the Minister's approval of the plan is required. In this way standards can be maintained, extravagances curtailed and representations and objections from interested parties considered.

Directions

Section 35 of the Town and Country Planning Act 1971 gives the Secretary of State for the Environment power to give directions to local planning authorities requiring that applications for permission to develop land (or all applications of a particular class) must be referred to him instead of being dealt with by the local authority. While this power – which effectively removes a great deal of autonomy from local authorities – is often used, others such as the powers to give directions under section 8 of the Clean Air Act 1968 (smoke-control programmes), section 72 of the Public Health Act 1936 (removal of house refuse), and section 29 of the Highways Act 1959 (public path creation orders), are not. In all cases these directions are issued to particular authorities.

Consents and Confirmations

Circular 5/60 of the Department of the Environment lays down that a local authority cannot sell a house built with the aid of a subsidy unless the Secretary of State gives his consent. This is one of a number of cases in which a Minister exercises control by grant of consents.

Similarly, no local by-laws can be effective until they are confirmed by a Minister. In this instance the control is absolute since by-laws are penal in nature, so it is necessary for the Minister to examine the by-law for legal validity. He will also wish to be assured that the by-law is *necessary* in the locality. Such control is vital since local by-laws may be challenged in the courts on the grounds of unreasonableness, repugnancy with statute or common law, uncertainty, or because it is *ultra vires* the authority. As far as good-rule and government by-laws are concerned they may also be challenged on the ground that a summary remedy already exists to prevent or suppress the nuisance at which the by-law is aimed.

Other Ministerial Controls

There are various miscellaneous forms of control available to Ministers of the Crown, other than those noted above. Ministers have an appellate jurisdiction: applicants for planning permission who are 'aggrieved' by the local planning authority's decision can appeal to the Secretary of State for the Environment under section 36 of the Town and Country Planning Act 1971; there is also a right of appeal under section 207 of the Highways Act 1959.

Under some Acts, such as the Coast Protection Act 1949 (section 36), Ministers are empowered to hold enquiries and demand information; this is effectively another form of Ministerial control. District auditors appointed to audit local authority accounts must be approved by the

Secretary of State, but he will not be questioned in Parliament as to their findings.

Some controls formerly exercised over local authorities by Ministers of the Crown were removed by the Local Government Act 1972 and the Local Government Act 1974, so the trend can be said to be towards a relaxation of central control by the Departments of State.

JUDICIAL CONTROL OF LOCAL AUTHORITIES

The courts have jurisdiction over local authorities in the same way as over individuals: the rules of contract and tort and crime may be applied equally to the man in the street and the local authority (except for certain obvious exceptions). In addition to this, however, the courts have a *supervisory* jurisdiction over the local authorities in respect of their activities, as they do over other executive agencies. The jurisdiction is called into play only where an aggrieved party commences an action, and in dealing with the matter the courts may grant a prerogative order, issue a declaration or injunction, or hear appeals where a right of appeal is conferred by statute.

The Prerogative Orders

Before 1938 prerogative writs could issue out of the High Court of Justice to compel inferior courts or officials to carry out their functions in accordance with the law or prevent them from exceeding the limits of their proper spheres of action. The writs were supplanted by the prerogative orders by virtue of section 7 of the Administration of Justice (Miscellaneous Provisions) Act 1938 which gave the High Court power to make orders of mandamus, prohibition and certiorari.

Mandamus. Where a local authority fails to carry out a duty which has been placed upon it by statute, or by common law, it may be compelled to perform that duty by the order of mandamus, which issues out of the High Court. Before the High Court will issue such an order certain conditions must be fulfilled however:

(1) The duty placed on the local authority must be an absolute one. If it is within the discretion of the authority to perform the duty or not no order of mandamus will lie. Thus, it could not be used to force the local authority to make improvement grants under section 2 of the Housing Act 1969, for this power is discretionary. It *can* lie to force the

exercise of the discretion, one way or the other; it can also issue to compel exercise of a discretionary power so as to exclude considerations extraneous to the performance of the duty.

(2) The order will be made only upon the application of a person who shows that he has a substantial personal interest in the duty being performed. In *R. v. Hereford Corporation* ex p. *Harrower* (1970) electrical contractors on a local authority's approved list applied for a mandamus directing the authority to comply with standing orders concerning public advertisement and public tender; it was held they had a legal right to apply for the order, *not as contractors*, but as ratepayers. In general, the element of 'substantiality' of interest is not easily categorised from the decided cases.

(3) The order will not be made if there is some other remedy available, which is equally convenient, just as beneficial, and as effective as mandamus would be. This is particularly the case if a statute specifically provides a remedy for the wrong complained of. No such other remedy was available in *R. v. Poplar Borough Council* (1922) where the council refused to pay sums under precepts issued by the London County Council and the Metropolitan District Asylums Board, so mandamus lay to compel the council to levy a rate to meet the precepts – there was no other effective means of ensuring the public duty was performed.

Although the order of mandamus is derived from the old prerogative writ of the same name it is now also available in a statutory form. Some statutes specifically provide that the Secretary of State can use mandamus to compel performance of duties given by the enabling Act. Whether derived from the common law or from statute the mandamus order carries an inherent penalty – the local authority which disobeys the order will find that its individual members who are responsible for the disobedience will be liable to attachment: they may be arrested and imprisoned until the order is obeyed.

Prohibition. The order of prohibition issues from the High Court to prevent an inferior court from exceeding the limits of its legitimate power, or from acting unlawfully. It thus restrains an inferior court from completing an act it has already commenced doing. The order lies against any body of persons having a duty in law to act in a judicial capacity. In *Ridge v. Baldwin* (1964) it was held that where a tribunal sits to decide a question affecting the rights of subjects it is then in a position where it must act judicially. Thus, in any situation where a local authority is called upon to 'determine questions affecting the rights of subjects' it accordingly acts in a judicial or quasi-judicial capacity and the order of prohibition may lie against it if it acts *ultra vires*, or otherwise unlawfully. It may be, for example, that the authority disregards the principles of natural justice (see below, page 39).

Certiorari. This order issues out of the High Court to enable a decision that has already been made by an inferior court, or other body acting in a judicial or quasi-judicial capacity, to be reviewed and, if necessary, quashed. It effectively calls the matter up to the High Court for review. In *R. v. Hendon Rural District Council,* ex p. *Chorley* (1933) the council approved a plan under section 4 of the Town Planning Act 1925, but one of the voting members had an interest in the development. Since the approval gave a legal right to compensation and thus affected the 'rights of subjects' it was held to be quasi-judicial in character, could thus be subject to certiorari, and since bias was present in the interested member the decision of the Council was quashed.

Certiorari will also lie where the body acting in a judicial or quasi-judicial capacity reaches a decision which discloses, on the face of the record, an error in law. In a 1952 case the reasons given by the Northumberland Compensation Appeal Tribunal showed that it had taken an erroneous view of the law and it was held that the fact it had yet acted within its jurisdiction was irrelevant – the order of certiorari could issue. If a decision were published without reasons given, of course, it is more difficult to challenge by certiorari but section 12 of the Tribunals and Inquiries Act 1971 plugged that particular loop-hole by enacting that tribunals listed in Schedule 1 of the Act must furnish a statement of reasons if called upon to do so by a person primarily concerned. This applies also to any Minister notifying a decision after a statutory enquiry. Such statements of reasons can be refused only on grounds of national security.

Natural Justice

Reference has been made to the term 'natural justice'. The principles of natural justice have not been enacted; 'the requirements of natural justice must depend on the circumstances of the case, the nature of the enquiry, the rules under which the tribunal is acting, the subject-matter under consideration and so forth' (Tucker L.J.). Nevertheless, the courts have laid down certain guidelines to follow in a number of decisions, and these can be summarised as three:

(*a*) the decision must be reached fairly, without bias, and in good faith;

(*b*) all parties concerned with the case must have been given a reasonable opportunity to put their cases to the tribunal;

(*c*) the tribunal must not act as a judge in its own cause.

There has been a recent tendency on the part of the judges to talk of the need for tribunals to act 'fairly' rather than merely to speak of 'fair hearings', so the principles of natural justice would now seem to be applied not only to clearly judicial decisions but also a rather wider range of administrative decisions. In *R. v. Sunderland Corporation* (1911) bias was successfully claimed where the justices, who were members of the borough council and who had actively supported the proposal out of which the action arose, were shown to have given a decision against the complainant. *Broadbent v. Rotherham Corporation* (1917) provides an example of the *audi alteram partem* rule. The corporation had made a demolition order under section 18 of the Housing and Town Planning Act 1909 and refused to consider an application for postponement, arguing it was useless to hear the plaintiff since no repairs could make the premises fit for human habitation. It was held to be wrong in its refusal; it was bound to act judicially in exercising its powers under the Act and so it should have heard the plaintiff before reaching a decision.

The limits of judicial control are such that the courts cannot be regarded as courts of appeal from 'judicial' bodies. They cannot review evidence and decide whether a correct decision has been arrived at, and in the absence of some express statutory provision conferring a right of appeal the functions of the courts are merely to see that jurisdiction has not been exceeded and that the principles of natural justice have been complied with. Indeed, some statutes expressly exclude judicial controls of this kind.

Declarations and Injunctions

A party who argues that an act or decision of a local authority is illegal may bring an action in the High Court for

(*a*) a declaration to that effect, or

(*b*) an injunction calling upon the authority to stop acting illegally, or

(*c*) a declaration coupled with an injunction.

These proceedings are available wherever a right is infringed, or where the rules of natural justice have been broken, or where the act of the authority is *ultra vires*, or an error of law is disclosed in the act or decision. By a declaratory judgment the court makes a statement on a question of law or rights; an injunction is an order directing a party to do, or stop doing, a particular thing.

The action is nominally commenced at the instigation of the Attorney-General since in theory public rights are involved; he sues 'at the relation of' the party actually aggrieved. But the Local Government Act 1972 enables an authority to institute civil proceedings in its own name so no *relator* action is necessary. Additionally, a private person can sue in his own name if the interference with the *public* right also interferes with his private right, and he can also sue in his own name if he suffers special damage over and above that arising from the interference with the public right. In *Boyce v. Paddington Corporation* (1903) the special damage arose from obstruction of light to Boyce's windows; in *Ridge v. Baldwin* (1964) the private right was the fact that the plaintiff chief constable had been dismissed by the Watch Committee, after criminal proceedings in which he had been acquitted of conspiracy to obstruct the course of public justice.

Declaratory judgments lie within the discretion of the court; if no useful purpose would be served by making the declaration the court will refuse to make it, as in *Bennett v. Chappell* (1966) where the plaintiff relied on a point of procedure to prevent a sale of land but when the hearing came on the land had already been lawfully conveyed.

Rights of Appeal

The Public Health Act 1961, like many other statutes, gives a right of appeal to the magistrates' court. By section 27 of the Act when a local authority requires an owner of a ruinous building to repair or demolish it the owner may appeal to the magistrates' court.

Rights of appeal also lie to a county court under some statutes, such as the Housing Act 1957 (sections 11 and 20) and the Highways Act 1959 (section 81). Section 59 of the Highways Act 1959 gives a right of appeal to the Crown Court but this is an exceptional situation, as is the right of appeal to the High Court under the Acquisition of Land (Authorisation Procedures) Act 1946. Normally appeals lie to the magistrates' courts.

In some cases a court is empowered to make its own discretionary decision in place of the discretion of the local authority – the question of whether proposed private street works are unreasonable is an example commonly given: the court can decide upon the question of reasonableness.

In any case, the courts will allow a hearing only where the person applying has 'standing' in the eyes of the court. Statutes often specify who may start proceedings in actions arising under the statute – usually, the 'person aggrieved' is nominated as one whose legal rights have been infringed or whose interests have been affected prejudicially. Where the prerogative orders of prohibition and certiorari are applied for the applicant will normally be one of the parties to the judicial or quasi-judicial proceeding which is complained of; as we have already seen ratepayers can bring actions against local authorities for declarations concerning the legality of the local authorities' acts. The whole situation regarding 'standing' has been criticised by the Law Commission, however, and it has been suggested that any person adversely affected by an act or omission by an administrative body should have the right to 'apply for review' of the act or omission to a court of law.

Administrative Discretion

It remains only to discuss the attitude of the courts towards the exercise of administrative discretion by local authorities. A case in point is *Meade v. Brighton Corporation* (1968). *M* applied for a permit to provide amusements with prizes under the Betting, Gaming and Lotteries Act 1963, which Act laid down no directions as to how the local authority should exercise its discretion in allowing the permit. The corporation refused the application. On appeal it was held that, although the Act gave a wide discretion to the local authority, that discretion must be exercised fairly and not by taking into account improper considerations.

Again, in *Padfield v. Minister of Agriculture, Fisheries and Food* (1968) it was held that where a statute gives a Minister discretion in the exercise of a power and does not limit or define the extent of the discretion or require him to give reasons for failing to exercise it, he must not, nevertheless, use his discretion in such a way that the objects of the statute in conferring the discretion are frustrated. He must exercise his discretion lawfully, must not misdirect himself in law, nor take account of irrelevant matters, nor omit relevant matters from consideration.

Authorities often lay down guidelines for themselves in the exercise of their discretionary powers. There is nothing legally objectionable in this provided the guidelines amount to a reasonable policy which it is fair and just to apply. But the policy must not be applied so rigidly as to reject an applicant without hearing what he has to say. 'The general rule is that anyone who has to exercise a statutory discretion must not "shut his ears to an application".' (Lord Reid in *British Oxygen Co. Ltd v. Minister of Technology* (1971).)

An authority can be compelled by mandamus to exercise a statutory discretion one way or the other, but what if a decision is taken on no evidence at all? The matter was raised in *Coleen Properties Ltd v. Minister of Housing and Local Government* (1971). The local authority obtained a compulsory purchase order under section 43(2) of the Housing Act 1957 but at a subsequent public local enquiry called no evidence as to the need to acquire the property. The Minister's inspector reported that the acquisition was not reasonably necessary and recommended its exclusion but the Minister rejected the recommendation and confirmed the order. Lord Denning said the Minister's decision was *ultra vires*: '. . . the mere *ipse dixit* of the local council is not sufficient. There must be some evidence to support their assertion.'

It may be added, as far as judicial control is concerned, that in all cases it can neither make new law nor consider policy. Its function is strictly limited: the courts can, at most, prevent the excessive use, or the misuse, of powers, or compel the proper performance of duties placed upon administrative authorities.

Judicial Review of Public Enquiries

It may be useful at this point to illustrate the stages by which a judicial review might be undertaken of a public local enquiry.

In *B. Johnson & Co. (Builders) Ltd v. Minister of Health* (1947) the owners of land subjected to a compulsory purchase order confirmed by the Minister applied to have the order quashed on the ground that the objectors had not received certain information given to the Minister by the local authority. The Court of Appeal held that the Minister was not bound to produce material obtained by him before the time for lodging of objections to the compulsory purchase order. This case shows how the judges make concessions to the realities of administration – the first step is the preparation of papers and reports to the local authority to persuade it to make the order; such materials cannot be made subject to inspection by aggrieved parties. They would be able to do so only if the material was produced as evidence at the enquiry.

Proceedings at public enquiries are subject to codes laid down by statutory instruments enacted on the recommendations of the Franks Committee on Tribunals and Enquiries. But these codes cannot cover all contingencies, and in some cases enquiries are not covered by such codes. It is in such instances that the courts sometimes make a review of the proceedings. Thus, in *T. A. Miller Ltd v. Minister of Housing and Local Government* (1946) the court was called upon to pronounce that the admission of hearsay evidence in the form of a letter to the public enquiry did not take away the applicant's right to a hearing since they had had the opportunity to comment on and contradict the material admitted. In *Charlton Sand & Ballast Co. v. Minister of Housing and Local Government* (1964), on the other hand, the court intervened to quash a Ministerial decision on the ground that the Minister had accepted an argument that was never raised at the enquiry, and the applicants had had no chance to give evidence on the matter in issue.

Once the public enquiry is over, the question of the report, and consultation between government departments, arises. Here again the courts will intervene. In *Lavender & Son v. Minister of Housing and Local Government* (1970) the final decision was in effect dictated by the Minister of Agriculture and the court quashed it on the principle of *delegatus non potest delegare.* Equally, a consultation between the Minister and the local authority, behind the backs of the objectors, will cause the courts to intervene, though in *Darlassis v. Minister of Education* (1954) it was held that if the consultation is on a matter of policy and with a government department which is not a party to the dispute with the landowner there is no breach of natural justice, and consequently no interference by the court. Rule 12(2) of SI 1092/1969 gives the applicant in a planning appeal the right to have the public enquiry reopened if the Minister disagrees with his inspector on a finding of fact and this tends to underline the care with which the courts approach the issue of *audi alteram partem* and the principle of natural justice.

This is not to say that the courts do not accept that a Minister must make a final independent judgment attaching such weight to his inspector's report as he thinks fit. There was a Ministerial rejection of the inspector's report in *Vale Estates (Acton) Ltd v. Secretary of State for the Environment* (1971) but the court refused to interfere, for the applicants had not established that the Minister had acted as 'no Minister acting reasonably could or should'.

In any event the statutory power for the courts to hear appeals from Ministerial decisions is limited strictly to points of law; in *Green v. Minister of Housing and Local Government* (1948) it was held that the courts are not permitted to hold a rehearing of the primary facts in issue.

LOCAL ADMINISTRATION COMMISSIONERS

One further method of control might be mentioned. A Parliamentary Commissioner is already part of the administrative machine as is the Health Service Commissioner. A new kind of local 'ombudsman' appeared under Part III of the Local Government Act 1974: the Act provided for the appointment of a Commission for Local Administration in England and another for Wales. The Local Commissioners have the duty of investigating complaints of maladministration in their areas.

The first avenue for the aggrieved person will still be the councillor, but if this fails and the complaint is of prejudice, or unfairness, incompetence or undue delay – or failure to do anything at all – a complaint can be made to the Local Commissioner through a member of the elected authority complained about. Only where a person cannot get a councillor to pass on the complaint will the Commissioner deal directly with the matter. He will in any case expect the local authority to have the opportunity to look into the matter themselves first, before he is called upon to act.

The Commissioner sends a report of his investigation and findings to the complainant, the councillor concerned, to the person complained of and the local authority. An annual general report is submitted to the Commissions, who are called upon to review annually the operation of this part of the Act.

Apart from county councils and borough and district councils (metropolitan and non-metropolitan) the Commissioner can also deal with complaints against water authorities and local authority police authorities in respect of administrative matters. The local authorities in London are also included within the Commissioner's jurisdiction.

A Local Commissioner is precluded from investigating:
  (a) an action regarding which the complainant has or has had a right of appeal to a statutory tribunal;
  (b) an action in respect of which a right of appeal exists (or existed) to a Minister;
  (c) an action in respect of which the aggrieved person has or has had a remedy in law.

Even so, though he is generally precluded, if the Commissioner is satisfied that in the particular circumstances it was not reasonable to expect the complainant to have taken advantage of the remedies open to him, the Commissioner may conduct an investigation.

The Commissioner is similarly precluded from investigating situations where the complainant claims to have suffered from a decision affecting the public at large, and in addition he may not look into those cases mentioned in Schedule 5 to the Act, which include legal proceedings, certain commercial transactions, the investigation of criminal behaviour, and matters relating to appointments of personnel, pay, discipline and other personal matters.

3

The Law of Housing

An important aspect of the work undertaken by local authorities is that in respect of housing. The law relating to housing is principally contained in the Housing Act 1957, the House Purchase and Housing Act 1959 and the Housing Acts of 1961, 1964, 1969 and 1972. The Housing Finance Act 1972 is also of importance as is the Housing (Amendment) Act 1973.

The responsibility for the administration of housing law is given to district councils and metropolitan districts and the Common Council in the City of London, while in Greater London the responsibility is divided between the Greater London Council and the London boroughs. County councils have certain powers regarding the provision of housing accommodation (see page 47). In general the responsibility of the authorities is to carry out periodic reviews to discover what action is necessary to provide housing accommodation and to deal with unsatisfactory housing conditions and slum clearance. Since 1974 the authorities have also had responsibility for housing homeless people. The work of the authorities is supervised by the Secretary of State for the Environment, who is empowered to issue default orders where authorities fail to discharge functions under the Housing Finance Act 1972, and may cause local inquiries to be held for the purpose of his powers and duties under the Housing Act 1957.

Representations on the practical working of the statutory provisions relating to housing can be made to the Secretary of State by the Central Housing Advisory Committee, whose advice he may seek.

The main areas of responsibility may now be dealt with.

PROVISION OF HOUSING ACCOMMODATION

All housing authorities must review housing conditions in their areas at periodic intervals, having regard, additionally, to the needs of the sick and chronically disabled. The powers to provide accommodation are laid down in section 92 of the Housing Act 1957: the authorities may acquire houses, erect houses on authority-owned land, convert, alter, enlarge, repair or improve housing or buildings acquired, and this may be done within or without the authorities' areas.

The housing authorities may also provide shops, recreation grounds and other amenities to serve its housing estates, with the prior approval of the Secretary of State; but his consent is not necessary to sell furniture to council-house tenants, provide laundries and meal or refreshment facilities.

If the periodic review is not carried out the Secretary of State may direct such a review to be undertaken. But reserve powers are also given to county councils, by section 194 of the Local Government Act 1972: they may provide accommodation for district councils, with the consent of the Secretary of State, who may make conditions for such an arrangement, particularly with regard to expenditure, ownership and management.

The general management and control of council houses lies with the housing authority, through by-laws and tenancy agreements, but in *Attorney-General v. Crayford Urban District Council* (1962) Pennycuick J. said: 'the power of the authority [under section 111 of the Housing Act 1957] is to manage its houses and the authority is limited to such acts as may fairly be regarded as acts of management by a landlord of his property in the ordinary sense of that term'.

The provision of accommodation may be undertaken by Housing Associations whom the authority may assist by making grants or loans, with the consent of the Secretary of State. By section 1 of the Housing Act 1964 the Housing Corporation was created with power to promote and assist the development of housing societies. The Housing Corporation may acquire land for these societies by compulsory purchase.

Rents

Council-dwelling rents had to be 'fair rents' in accordance with the Housing Finance Act 1972. The Act did not define a fair rent but stated that regard had to be paid to all the circumstances (other than the tenant's means) and in particular the age, character, locality and state of repair of the dwelling. Market demand was ignored and tenant improvements disregarded unless made pursuant to the terms of the tenancy. Disrepair or defects arising from a tenant's failure to comply with the tenancy terms were also to be disregarded in fixing the fair rent.

Lists of fair rents were published by authorities when the Act came into force and were to be subject to triennial review. The application of the fair rent principle to local authority dwellings was brought to an end by the Housing Rents and Subsidies Act 1975. This Act released the local authorities and the new town corporations from the duty to charge rents in accordance with the 1972 Act. Instead, local authorities were called upon to charge reasonable rents, in accordance with Part V of the Housing Act 1957. The Act also requires the authorities to review these rents from time to time. Section 1 of the Act also makes provision for reasonable working balances in the Housing Revenue Accounts of local authorities and local authorities are not to provide for a surplus.

Section 2 of the Act deals with the limitation of rent increases in the public sector. The Secretary of State is empowered to make orders limiting such increases, not by reference to individual local authorities or new town corporations, but generally, or by reference to specified descriptions of authorities, corporations or dwellings.

Rent rebate schemes must be operated by all housing authorities, complying with Schedules 3 and 4 of the Housing Finance Act 1972. The provisions of these schedules can be varied by statutory instruments issued by the Secretary of State. Authorities can depart from the schedules but tenants must in such circumstances receive treatment as favourable as the conditions applying in the model scheme. A permitted total payment is laid down for rent rebates – the amount which would have been paid had the model scheme been followed plus 10 per cent is the total beyond which an amended scheme cannot go.

By section 113(2) of the Housing Act 1957 housing authorities must give reasonable preference, in its selection of tenants, to persons living in insanitary or overcrowded houses, to those who have large families and to those who live under unsatisfactory conditions. It should be noted that the security-of-tenure provisions of the Rent Act 1968 do not apply to council-dwelling tenants.

DISPOSAL AND PURCHASE PROVISIONS

By section 104 of the Housing Act 1957 housing authorities can, with the general or specific consent of the Secretary of State, sell or lease houses provided by them under Part V of the Act. They may impose such covenants and conditions as they think fit regarding the use and maintenance of the houses and can accept instalment payments or agree for payment by mortgage. Conditions may also be imposed as to:

(*a*) a price limit at which the house may be sold during any period not exceeding five years from completion of the sale;

(*b*) a rent limit if the house is let during the five-year period;

(*c*) a ban on selling the house or letting it during the five-year period after completion of purchase from the authority, unless notification is given to the authority with an offer to sell back to the authority.

The Housing (Financial Provisions) Act 1958 introduced a scheme whereby advances can be made by the authorities to persons to enable them to acquire or build houses, to convert buildings into houses, and to carry out the enlargement, repair and improvement of houses. The advance will be secured by mortgage and may be up to the full value of the property. The property itself may be of any value, but it must be freehold or leasehold with at least ten years to run beyond the period of the loan. The Act also gives housing authorities power to guarantee repayments to a building society for an advance by the society, but the guarantee scheme must be approved by the Secretary of State.

A somewhat older provision by which housing authorities may lend money is found in the Small Dwellings Acquisition Acts 1899–1923, whereby advances up to a full market value of £5000 may be made. Conditions attaching to such loans cover prompt payment, insurance and the continued residence of the borrower in the house. The conditions may be enforced by sale, or taking possession of the house (if the condition as to residence is broken).

Under the Housing Act 1969 housing authorities can make advances repayable on maturity or on the happening of a specified event – such as the sale of the property – before the end of the period of the loan. Such loans can be made to alter, enlarge, repair or improve a dwelling.

GRANTS FOR IMPROVEMENT AND CONVERSION

Three different kinds of grants are available for improvements and conversions: improvement grants, standard grants and special grants.

Improvement Grants

Housing authorities may make improvement grants for alteration and enlargement and repairs and replacements incidental to an improvement or needed to make an improvement fully effective. The dwelling must conform to the 'twelve-point standard' however (see page 50), and the cost involved must exceed £100 (or other prescribed amount). Additionally, no grant will be made where the costs of repair and replacement make up more than half of the approved expenses, and in any case the authority must be satisfied that the dwelling will provide satisfactory housing accommodation for thirty years (or shorter period not less than ten years in justifiable circumstances). Also, the applicant for a grant must have a fee-simple interest in the property or a leasehold interest with at least five years to run.

The Twelve-point Standard. This is the standard prescribed by the Secretary of State; it must be met after improvement or conversion where an improvement grant is applied for. The standard demands that the dwelling must, after improvement or conversion:

(1) be in a good state of repair and substantially free from damp;
(2) have an adequate supply of wholesome water laid on inside the dwelling;
(3) be provided with efficient and adequate means of supplying hot water for domestic purposes;
(4) have an internal water closet or, if this is not practicable, have a readily accessible outside water closet;
(5) have a fixed bath or shower in a bathroom;
(6) be provided with a sink or sinks and with suitable arrangements for the disposal of waste water;
(7) have a proper drainage system;
(8) be provided in each room with adequate points for gas or electric lighting (where reasonably available);
(9) be provided with adequate facilities for heating;
(10) have each room properly lighted and ventilated;
(11) have satisfactory facilities for storing, preparing and cooking food;
(12) have proper provision for storing fuel (where required).

Where an authority considers it impracticable to insist on any of these requirements it can dispense with it.

The grant towards the approved expenses of the proposed works must not exceed one-half of the expenses or £1000 per dwelling, whichever is the less. The limit for conversion of a house of three or more storeys is £1200.

Standard Grants

Standard grants may be payable where a dwelling lacks 'standard amenities' such as:

fixed bath (or shower)	£30
hot- and cold-water supply at a fixed bath or shower	£45
wash hand basin	£10
hot- and cold-water supply at a wash hand basin	£20
sink	£15
hot- and cold-water supply at sink	£30
water closet	£50

Additional sums may be payable where a piped-water supply or sewerage facilities are to be provided, but the total must not exceed £450.

Before a standard grant is payable (and it cannot in any case be paid for a house built after 2 October 1961) the housing authority must be satisfied that the work to be done will provide the dwelling with standard amenities for the exclusive use of the occupants, be in good repair and fit for human habitation. The authority must be satisfied in addition, that the dwelling has at least fifteen years' useful life and the applicant must have a fee-simple interest or a leasehold interest with at least five years to run.

By a direction in Circular 64/69 the authority can give approval for a standard grant even though these conditions are not fulfilled – provided that in certain cases the consent of the Secretary of State is first obtained.

Special Grants

Special grants are payable towards works required to provide standard amenities for a house in multiple occupation. The grant will equal one-half of the total cost of providing each of the standard amenities as above for each family unit. The approval is discretionary, subject to directions which the Secretary of State may give.

Where a special grant has been made the authority can fix a time limit (not less than twelve months) within which the work is to be completed, and this provision applies equally to improvement and standard grants. Grants may not be approved if works are already begun unless the authority is satisfied there was good reason for this. Where the authority refuses approval of any of these grants, or fixes less than the maximum for an improvement grant, it must give its reasons in writing if requested to do so by the applicant.

By section 16 of the Housing Act 1969 the Secretary of State is under a duty to make an annual contribution towards the authority's expenditure in making these grants. The contribution equals three-quarters of the annual loan charges for a period of twenty years. He may also pay contributions towards the cost incurred on conversion or improvement in circumstances similar to those in which an improvement grant or standard grant might be payable.

General Improvement Areas

A housing authority is empowered to declare as a general improvement area any area predominantly residential in character where living conditions should be improved by the improvement of amenities or dwellings, or where this ought to be done by the authority. Land comprising a clearance area under Part III of the Housing Act 1957 cannot be so designated. The powers of the authority in general improvement areas cover both houses and environment generally. It may carry out work on its own land or assist in work on land belonging to others; acquire land by agreement; let or dispose of its own land; and with the consent of the Secretary of State acquire land by compulsory purchase within the designated area or adjoining it. If it buys land under this power it must rehouse displaced persons.

Improvement grants are payable in these areas, but standard grants are discretionary since the area plan should bring up the dwellings to the twelve-point standard.

The Secretary of State may pay a contribution towards the approved expenditure of the authority under the scheme. The approved expenditure may not, in the aggregate, exceed £200 for each dwelling in the general improvement area, or for each dwelling which will be in the area when finally improved.

UNFIT HOUSES AND CLEARANCE AREAS

Part II of the Housing Act 1957 deals with the repair, maintenance and sanitary conditions of houses, with supplementary provisions in sections 24 to 26 of the Housing Act 1961. The standard of fitness laid down in the 1957 Act states nine factors which must be taken into account: repair; stability; freedom from damp; internal arrangement; natural lighting; ventilation; water supply; drainage and sanitary convenience; facilities for preparation and cooking of food and for the disposal of waste water. A house will be deemed unfit only if it is defective in one or more of these matters, so defective that it is not reasonably suitable for occupation in that condition.

If the authority is satisfied that a house is unfit for human habitation but the defects can be remedied at reasonable cost the person who has control of the house may be served with a notice requiring him to undertake the repairs. His failure to carry out the work may lead to the authority doing it instead, thereafter recovering the expenses from him, with interest, in the county court or magistrates' court if necessary. The authority may declare the expenses payable by instalments and declare outstanding payments a charge on the property. If an appeal is made, and a court holds that the house is not capable of repair at reasonable cost, the authority may purchase the house by agreement or compulsorily.

Alternatively, the authority itself may consider the house to be beyond repair at reasonable cost. It may then serve a notice upon the person having control of the premises, the owner and every mortgagee, inviting representations from them regarding the condition and future use of the house and the proposed repairs to it. An undertaking to repair may be given to the authority with a list of proposed works; if it is not given and accepted the authority can make a demolition order or a closing order preventing the house or part of it being used for human habitation. Underground rooms can be made subject to a closing order if the average height of the room, floor to ceiling, is not at least seven feet or the room does not otherwise comply with the authority's regulations concerning underground rooms. Houses will be made subject to closure orders rather than demolition orders if

(*a*) adjoining houses are in a state of good repair or if

(*b*) they are of historic interest.

The owner served with a demolition order must pull down the house within the time prescribed, otherwise the authority may do so and sell the materials. A right of appeal to the county court within twenty-one days of the making of the demolition order, closing order or notice of intention to purchase may be claimed.

The problem for the housing authority may be not that there is a house unfit for human habitation to be dealt with but a *number* of such houses grouped together. In such circumstances the authority may make a clearance area declaration. To declare an area a clearance area –

the so-called 'pink' land – the authority must be satisfied as to certain matters laid down in section 42 of the Housing Act 1957. These are:

(1) that the houses (which can include tenements, or a garage or workshop with dwellings above) are unfit for human habitation or are, by reason of their bad arrangement, or the narrowness or bad arrangement of the streets, dangerous or injurious to the health of the inhabitants of the area, and that other buildings, if any, in the area are for like reason dangerous or injurious to the health of the inhabitants; and

(2) that the most satisfactory way of dealing with the conditions in the area is to demolish all the buildings in the area; and

(3) that alternative accommodation can be made available; and

(4) that the authority's resources are sufficient.

After the clearance area is declared the authority can make a clearance order, calling upon the owners to clear the site or else it can buy the land and carry out the demolition itself. The decision is a discretionary one: in *Robins v. Minister of Health* (1939) the brewers, who protested that they were able and willing to carry out the demolition themselves and a compulsory purchase order was not necessary, discovered that in the court's view it was entirely up to the authority to decide which course to take.

Notice of the clearance order is publicised and served on all owners, mortgagees, lessees and occupiers in order that objections may be lodged. If objections are made the Secretary of State must hold a public local inquiry, or give the objectors a hearing before he confirms the clearance order. Once confirmed, the confirmation must be publicised in the local press and the objectors also must be informed. Any person aggrieved by the order then has the right to challenge it in the High Court as *ultra vires* the Act or on the ground that some requirement of the Act has not been complied with.

The order becomes effective after six weeks from publication of the confirmation, if no High Court action has been started.

By section 44 of the Housing Act 1957 failure on the part of the owners to demolish the buildings can lead to the work being done by the authority, who may then sell the materials and recover any outstanding balance from the owners as a simple contract debt. A surplus will be returned to the owners. If the owners do demolish, but do not develop the land within eighteen months thereafter, the authority can purchase the land by agreement or compulsorily.

Postponement of demolition is possible where the authority is satisfied the houses can be made capable of providing accommodation of an adequate standard for the time being, and under the Housing Act 1961 an authority can ask the Secretary of State to take a house or houses out of the clearance order if the authority is satisfied the property in question is or can be made fit to live in. But temporary occupation under the Housing Acts does not lend statutory authority to the use of a house prejudicial to health: *Salford City Council v. McNally* (1975).

As an alternative to making a clearance order the authority can buy the land by agreement or under compulsory purchase powers. Adjacent land can also be acquired if this is necessary for satisfactory development (this is known as 'grey' land).

Compensation

If the authority compulsorily acquires a house unfit for human habitation the amount of compensation due to the owner is the value of the cleared site; it cannot exceed the market value of the site with the property on it. This rule is modified:

(*a*) if the house was used for business purposes – a claim for compensation for receipts from the business may be made;

(*b*) if the property was well maintained during the five years previous to the compulsory purchase order – an additional payment equal to four times the rateable value may be made but it must not exceed the difference between the full compulsory purchase value and the site value;

(*c*) if the compensation comes to less than the gross value of the house it is made up to the gross value;

(*d*) if the house is owner-occupied full compensation is payable provided the house has been continuously occupied since 23 April 1968 by the owner or a member of his family, or otherwise has been in such occupation for the two years before the commencement of the 'relevant proceedings' after being acquired for owner-occupation post-1968. The relevant proceedings are the declaration of a clearance order; and even though the above conditions do not apply full compensation is still payable to a purchaser in good faith within the qualifying period.

Where property other than condemned property is acquired the assessment of compensation follows general principles (see page 179). Where the authority proceeds by way of a clearance order, closing order or demolition order rather than by purchase no compensation is payable, though payments may be made in cases (*a*), (*b*) and (*d*) above. Well-maintained property under a closing order may give rise to an additional payment after inspection on behalf of the Secretary of State and a claim for such payment can be made, with appeal against refusal to the county court.

Circular 126/74 drew attention to the provisions of the Housing Act 1974 affecting clearance procedures in relation to unfit houses. An annex to the circular summarised the provisions laid down in Schedule 9 of the Housing Act 1974 and the Regulations prescribe the form in which notification to the owner, lessee, occupier or mortgagee must be made. A person entitled to notification in different capacities must be served with separate notices.

Section 60(1B) of the Housing Act 1957 requires authorities to give reasons in the notifications informing the recipient that the whole or part of the house has not been well maintained. The reasons must be given in sufficient detail and not in such broad terms as 'general disrepair'. 'Exterior' can be read to mean external items a landlord might be expected to keep in repair, such as guttering, main walls, roofs and outside drains. For a house falling within section 67(2) of the Housing Act 1969 'exterior' can also mean common staircases, halls, landings and parts occupied for business purposes.

A person wishing to make written representations against the authority's decision on maintenance must send such representations to the Secretary of State within the objections period of the relevant clearance, compulsory purchase or unfitness order. The prescribed forms for notification of maintenance require the insertion of a date before which objections must be made, as do the prescribed forms for the personal notices of the making of the orders. The minimum permissible period is fourteen days from the date of service of the notice. In practice, authorities are asked by Circular 126/74 to allow a minimum period of twenty-eight days in every case where this is possible.

By section 2 of the Housing (Slum Clearance) Compensation Act 1965 the jurisdiction of county courts to modify outstanding liabilities under mortgages, or agreements to purchase by instalments, in respect of unfit houses condemned or compulsorily purchased, was extended to owner-occupiers of unfit houses in general. Regard may be had, in addition, to whether the original price paid for the house was excessive.

OVERCROWDING AND MULTIPLE OCCUPATION

A duty is placed upon local authorities, by sections 76 and 77 of the Housing Act 1957, to inspect their areas for overcrowding and to submit to the Secretary of State proposals to abate such overcrowding. Occupiers or landlords who permit overcrowding, as defined by the Act, commit an offence which is punishable by fine. No offence is committed if the overcrowding occurs through a natural increase in the family, though again, liability will follow even in such circumstances if suitable alternative accommodation is offered and the family remains in overcrowded premises.

A landlord aware of overcrowding must inform the authority who may by licence temporarily allow a house to be overcrowded; under section 83 of the 1957 Act and section 17 of the Rent Act 1968 in some circumstances a landlord can obtain possession if the overcrowding is of the kind to make him liable. Where overcrowding exists an abatement order can be served by the housing authority; thereafter, if the overcrowding continues a court order may be obtained from the magistrates for vacant possession to be given to the landlord.

The question of multiple occupation is covered by the Housing Acts of 1961, 1964 and 1969. Housing authorities are compelled to register all houses in multiple occupation. By multiple occupation is meant the occupation of a house or part of a house by persons who do not form a single household. The housing authority is empowered to make a scheme for the registration of houses in multiple occupation; it may also prohibit multiple occupation of houses unless they are registered. The Secretary of State's code of management for such houses may be applied by the authority and it may insist upon the standards laid down in the code to be applied to the houses in multiple occupation in its area. The code covers repair, maintenance, cleansing, gas, water and electricity supplies, drainage, sanitary and washing facilities, common stairways, yards and outbuildings, disposal of refuse and litter, and fire-escape arrangements. The management order is registrable as a land charge.

Quite unrelated to the code of management an authority may demand work to be carried out on such matters as lighting and ventilation and fire escapes and may issue directions as to how many people are to be permitted to live in the house concerned. If living conditions in the house are so bad that immediate action is necessary in order that the safety, health and welfare of the residents should be protected a control order can be made. This gives the housing authority immediate control of the house. This order also is registrable as a land charge; appeal against the order lies to the county court. While the control order remains in force the authority holds all the rights of the dispossessed owner and must carry out works as though a management order had been made. It may collect rents from the occupiers, let vacant accommodation and must keep a strict account of its dealings. The order will expire after five years unless revoked by the authority, or by the court on appeal. The financial effect of the proposals for a control order must be communicated to the owner within eight weeks of the making of the order and he may appeal against the scheme envisaged to the county court.

Generally, in order to deal with deficiencies in houses in multiple occupation as far as amenities are concerned, the housing authority may stipulate a maximum number of individuals or households, or both, who may occupy a house.

FINANCE AND RENT CONTROL

By section 12 of the Housing Finance Act 1972 the housing authority must keep a housing revenue account of all income and expenditure in relation to housing provided under Part V of the Housing Act 1957. The detailed make-up of the account is dealt with in the First Schedule to the Act.

Housing authorities may borrow money for purposes connected with the repair and works to be undertaken upon houses under Part II of the 1957 Act; they may also borrow in connection with clearance orders under Part III of the Act, provision of accommodation under Part V and for the purposes of the Housing Act 1958. They may use the ordinary methods of borrowing (see page 32) and may, in addition, issue local housing bonds.

The system of exchequer contributions was rewritten in the Housing Finance Act 1972 with the introduction of various subsidies to cover housing, improvement and conversion and general improvement areas. The Housing Rents and Subsidies Act 1975 removed some of these subsidies, however: the residual subsidy, the transition subsidy, the rising costs subsidy, the operational deficit subsidy, the rent rebate subsidy and the town development subsidy were stated to be not payable for the year 1975–6 and after. The subsidies now available are as follows.

Subsidies

A *housing subsidy* is payable to local authorities and new town corporations, in accordance with Part 1 of Schedule I of the Housing

Rents and Subsidies Act 1975. The subsidy consists of five elements: a basic element, a new capital costs element, a supplementary financing element, a special element and a high costs element.

For 1975–6 and thereafter a *modified rent rebate* subsidy is payable to local authorities and new town corporations. The amount equals 75% of their standard amount of rent rebates for the year. Local authorities must make rate fund contributions each year equal to 25% of their standard amount of rent rebates for the year and the amount by which rent rebates granted by them exceed the standard amount and their costs of administering their rebate scheme under Part II of the Housing Finance Act 1972.

Expanding towns subsidies are payable in respect of 'qualifying dwellings' (provided for letting in a scheme of town development) for ten years from the time they are let to 'qualifying persons' (a person of the kind for whom such accommodation is necessary for the success of the scheme).

Where a town development subsidy was previously payable a *transitional town development subsidy* is payable for 1975–6 and thereafter. The subsidy can be reduced or discontinued where a dwelling is demolished, disposed of or unfit to be used, or other relevant circumstances apply. The decision lies with the Secretary of State whether to discontinue or reduce this subsidy.

Improvements and Conversions

Exchequer contributions may be payable to local authorities who make improvement grants, grants for standard amenities or special grants to provide standard amenities in houses in multiple occupation. By the Housing Act 1971 and the Housing (Amendment) Act 1973 higher grants and contributions are payable for house improvement in local authority areas wholly or partly within a development area as defined by section 1 of the Local Employment Act 1970.

General Improvement Areas

Expenditure incurred in general improvement areas by local authorities may give rise to exchequer contributions equal to one-half of the loan charges for twenty years. The approved expenditure must not exceed in aggregate £200 per dwelling in the general improvement area as defined.

Rent Control and Allowances

Housing authorities have the power to publish information for landlords, tenants and others concerning rights and duties arising under the Landlord and Tenant Act 1962, Part III of the Rent Act 1965 (protection from harassment and eviction), the Rent Act 1968 and Parts III, IV and VII and section 90 of the Housing Finance Act 1972. Proceedings under the Rent Act 1968 or under Part III of the Rent Act 1965 can be started by the authority.

Controlled Tenancies

A 'controlled tenancy' is an unfurnished tenancy beginning before 6 July 1957, in respect of a dwelling with a rateable value of not more than £40 in London or £30 elsewhere in England or Wales. On the application of a controlled tenant a local authority can issue a certificate of disrepair in respect of the dwelling; this will require an abatement of rent to a certain proportion until the certificate is cancelled.

Regulated Tenancies

A regulated tenancy is an unfurnished tenancy (other than a controlled tenancy) with a rateable value on 23 March 1955 of not more than £400 in Greater London and £200 elsewhere in England and Wales. The housing authority rent officers must register such tenancies in accordance with schemes made by the Secretary of State for each registration area. The rent officer must keep a register of rents and regulated tenancies and act as an intermediary between landlords and tenants in the determination of fair rents for registration. If they cannot agree, a rent assessment committee will determine the fair rent.

Since 1 July 1975, all controlled tenancies have become regulated tenancies.

Under Part VI of the Rent Act 1968 rent tribunals can determine the rent payable for furnished tenancies and give a limited security of tenure to the tenant. The local authority must keep a register for its area of rents so determined and may refer contracts for furnished tenancies to the tribunal.

Rent Allowances

Under Part II of the Housing Finance Act 1972 local authorities must operate rent-allowance schemes for private tenants under regulated and controlled tenancies. The Secretary of State can modify the model scheme set out in Schedule 3 of the Act and may allow a departure if the level of local authority rents or of private rents or of rents of any class of local authority or private dwellings is higher than the general level elsewhere.

Schemes may be varied but not so as to allow a person to receive a smaller allowance than he would have received under the model scheme. Total allowances granted in a year must not amount to more than 110% of the standard amount of rent allowances for the authority (that amount which the authority would pay out if it used the model scheme).

Housing Rents and Subsidies Act 1975

Apart from its provisions regarding subsidies the Act made certain changes as far as rents in the private and public sector are concerned. The machinery for determining rents for local authority and new town corporation dwellings, found in Parts V and VI of the Housing Finance Act 1972, was swept away, though the duties regarding rent-rebate schemes and rent-allowance schemes remained unaffected. Section 1(2) of the 1975 Act placed a duty upon local authorities to review rents from time to time and make such changes as are required by the circumstances.

Section 7 of the Act extended the phasing of rent increases provisions found in the Housing Act 1969 and the Housing Finance Act 1972 to those houses whose rent is registered and the tenancy is a regulated tenancy presently subsisting.

By section 8 of the Act certain amenities are to be disregarded in determining a fair rent. Section 9 stipulates that no controlled tenancy of a dwelling-house shall cease to be a controlled tenancy by reference to the rateable value of the house and by section 10 increases of rent under controlled tenancies are permitted towards the cost of repairs.

The power to make orders under section 11 of the Counter-Inflation Act 1973 restricting or preventing increases of rent was superseded by section 11 of the 1975 Act.

4

The Law of Public Health

Until legislation appeared in the nineteenth century bringing some
order into a situation bordering on the chaotic the regulation of public
health was not seen necessarily as a function of the State or of local
government. Indeed, one of the important methods of control was by
way of the law of nuisance, which placed the responsibility for action
squarely upon the individual. While nuisance still has a part to play
today, the Public Health Acts from 1875 onwards provide the basis for
the law relating to public health.

The authorities who are responsible for public health are district
councils, London borough councils, the Common Council and the
Under Treasurers of the Temples – for most of the functions, but
some, such as refuse-disposal, are discharged by county councils and
the Greater London Council, and others such as baths, wash-houses,
mortuaries and offensive ditches are the responsibility of parish and
community councils.

Joint boards and port health authorities also play their part and it is
open to the Secretary of State for Social Services to make an order
constituting a union of districts to be administered for public health
purposes by a joint board, subject to certain restrictions, and he may
constitute by order a port health authority for the area of a customs
port.

Powers given to an authority for health and sanitation purposes
cannot be used for purposes not connected with health and sanitation,
so in *Pilling v. Abergele Urban District Council* (1950) the council was held
to have acted wrongly in taking town planning considerations into
account when deciding whether or not to grant a licence under section
269 of the Public Health Act 1936. It should have had regard only to
matters relating to health and sanitation.

PROVISIONS RELATING TO BUILDINGS, SITES AND SANITATION

The regulation of the construction of buildings from the point of view of the environment and the prevention of danger from structural defects and fire dates back to the Public Health Act 1875 which gave urban authorities power to regulate the construction of new streets and new buildings by means of by-laws. These provisions were superseded by the Public Health Act 1936 which enabled local authorities to make by-laws relating to the construction, materials used and ventilation and so on of buildings, leaving the Public Health Act 1961, the Building Regulations 1972, the Fire Precautions Act 1971 and the London Government Act 1963 to cover the matters by way of the building regulations made by the Secretary of State for the Environment.

By section 64 of the Public Health Act 1936 persons undertaking work which comes within the provisions of the building regulations must submit plans to the authority, which *must* approve them if they are not defective and conform with the regulations. The Act[1] lays down specific grounds upon which an authority must reject plans:

(*a*) where a building is to be built over a sewer, unless the authority considers that consent can properly be given (section 25);

(*b*) where unsatisfactory provision is made for drainage (section 37) or sanitary accommodation (section 43);

(*c*) where building is to be carried out on ground filled with offensive materials (section 54);

(*d*) where there is insufficient access for the removal of refuse (section 55);

(*e*) in the case of public buildings, where satisfactory entrances and exits are not available (section 59, and section 30 of the Fire Precautions Act 1971);

(*f*) where there is unsatisfactory provision for a sufficient water supply (section 137 and Schedule 9 of the Water Act 1973);

(*g*) where the authority is not satisfied, in plans for buildings other than residences, shops and offices, that the height of chimneys is adequate (section 10 of the Clean Air Act 1956);

(*h*) in the case of industrial buildings, unless the buildings conform to insulation standards laid down by regulations (Thermal Insulation (Industrial Buildings) Act 1957 and Thermal Insulation (Industrial Buildings) Regulations 1972).

Apart from these grounds, on which the authority *must* reject plans submitted, there are circumstances where it *may* reject them. By section

31 of the Public Health Act 1961 plans for a house may be rejected if sufficient and suitable food-storage accommodation is not shown and, by section 33, if a bathroom with hot and cold water is not included.

The Public Health Acts also concern themselves with time limits. If the person depositing plans does not proceed with the building works within three years thereafter the authority can declare the deposit of no effect (section 66 of the Public Health Act 1936). If the building materials to be used are not suitable for long life the authority may fix a period at the end of which the building must be removed (subject to an extension of time being allowed), and it may also impose conditions on the use of the materials (section 53 of the Public Health Act 1936, and Schedule 1 to the Public Health Act 1961). The materials in question are specified in the building regulations.

Disputes may be determined by a court of summary jurisdiction or, if both parties agree, by reference to the Secretary of State for settlement.

Breach of the Building Regulations

Where building work is carried on in breach of the building regulations the local authority may demand that the owner pull down or alter work done. If the owner ignores the notice the authority itself may pull down, alter or remove the work and charge the cost of the operation to the person on whom the notice was served, provided the notice was served within twelve months of completion of the works.

It may be that the work as a whole was planned to conform to the regulations but individual parts of the building work do not; in such a case, it was held in *Sunley Homes Ltd v. Borg* (1969), proceedings may be taken before completion of the building in respect of the parts contravening the regulations. The Attorney-General or the authority or any other person may apply for an injunction for removal of or alteration to work contravening the building regulations, but the authority may be ordered to pay compensation to the owner where it then transpires that the work *was* completed in conformity with the regulations, as it may where notice of rejection was given by the authority within the prescribed time.

In any case it should be noted that the Secretary of State can, after consultation with the local authority, dispense with compliance with the regulations where he feels that the operation of the regulation would be unreasonable in the circumstances. Regulation A14 of the Building Regulations 1972 delegates the exercise of this dispensing power to the local authorities except in relation to their own applications. Unless the work affects an internal part of the building public notice of the dispensation must be given. If an application for relaxation of the regulations is not dealt with by the authority an appeal can be made to the Secretary of State, as it can where the authority refuses to grant what the applicant asks for (section 7, Public Health Act 1961).

In the First Schedule to the 1961 Act provision appears for relaxation in respect of certain cases of existing work to cover situations where the building regulations have been inadvertently contravened but this provision cannot be relied upon where the authority had become entitled to pull down, alter or remove the work under the enforcement rules of the Public Health Act 1936.

Dangerous Structures

By section 24 of the Public Health Act 1961 and section 58 of the 1936 Act where a structure is in a dangerous condition the authority can make application to a court of summary jurisdiction for an order compelling the owner to remedy the defects or otherwise demolish the building and remove the consequent rubbish. In default of action by the owner the authority can then carry out the work in the way it thinks fit and charge the cost to the owner. In addition the owner can be fined up to £10.

It may be that the structure is so dangerous that in the opinion of the authority immediate action is necessary. In such a case the authority must, if it is reasonably practicable, give notice to the owner and occupier and then take such steps as it deems necessary to end the danger, recovering the cost of the operation from the owner through the magistrates' court. It may then have to explain why such haste was necessary and why the ordinary procedures could not be followed.

Demolition

Section 29 of the Public Health Act 1961 deals with local authority powers regarding demolition. In general a person who wishes to demolish a building must first notify the authority, who may require that various safety measures should be taken, such as the shoring up of adjacent buildings, the weatherproofing of exposed surfaces and the sealing or removal of drains and pipes. The notice may be appealed against to the magistrates' court. If the person wishing to demolish does not comply with the terms of the notice the authority itself may carry out the precautionary measures and may, in addition or alternatively, take proceedings for recovery of a fine.

Ruinous Buildings

By section 27 of the 1961 Act, if a building is seriously detrimental to
the amenities of the neighbourhood because of its ruinous or
dilapidated condition, the authority may issue a notice requiring repair
or restoration work to be carried out – or, if the owner chooses,
demolition. Once again, in default of action by the owner the authority
may take the necessary steps itself, and may proceed for a fine.

Vacant Sites

A local authority may require the site on which a building has been
demolished to be cleared up and all rubbish removed. Equally,
authorities can take such steps for the removal of rubbish from vacant
sites as is considered necessary in the interests of amenity. Before action
can be taken the authority must serve a notice on the occupier or owner,
stating what it proposes to do; the recipient may serve a counter-notice
to the effect that he will take the necessary steps himself, or alternatively
he may appeal to the magistrates' court on the ground that the action of
the local authority is unjustified. Where a counter-notice has been
served the authority must wait to see if the steps are taken within a
reasonable time or, if work starts, that reasonable progress is made, in
the removal of the rubbish.[2]

Conservation Areas

By section 277A of the Town and Country Amenities Act 1974 the
demolition of buildings in conservation areas is brought under control
by applying, with modifications, the listed buildings control provisions
of the Act. Anyone wishing to demolish a building within a conservation
area must first apply for listed building consent to the local planning
authority (separately, or as part of an application for planning
permission for redevelopment). In assessing whether or not consent
should be forthcoming authorities must take account of the importance
of the building to the character or appearance of any part of the
conservation area. Circular 147/74 of the Department of the Environment stressed that the consent to demolish should be given, generally,
only where acceptable and detailed plans for redevelopment are
available. Local authorities seeking consent to demolish a building in a
conservation area must make application directly to the Secretary of
State.

Section 290(1) of the Act defines 'building' as including any part of a building and the Circular suggests that demolition of part would be regarded as demolition of a building for the purposes of section 277A.

The demolition control provisions do not apply to certain descriptions of buildings, such as:

(*a*) buildings with a cubic content not exceeding 115 metres;

(*b*) buildings within the curtilage of a dwelling-house, gates, fences, walls, temporary buildings, agricultural buildings, industrial buildings, erected in pursuance of a permission granted by Article 3 of the Town and Country General Development Order 1973;[3]

(*c*) a building required to be demolished by virtue of a discontinuance order under section 51, or of any provision of an agreement made under section 52 of the Town and Country Planning Act 1971;

(*d*) buildings in respect of which the requirements of an enforcement notice require its demolition, or which must be demolished by virtue of a condition of planning permission;

(*e*) buildings included under operative clearance orders or compulsory purchase orders;

(*f*) ecclesiastical buildings in respect of which a redundancy scheme has been drafted under the Pastoral Measure 1968.

Rubbish Dumps and Poisonous Waste

The county councils in England and district councils in Wales are under an obligation to provide places where refuse (other than refuse from business activity) might be deposited. To residents the service is free, but authorities may make a charge on others. Section 18 of the Civic Amenities Act 1967 also empowers district councils to remove abandoned vehicles and county councils in England and district councils in Wales to dispose of them. Penalties are imposed for the unauthorised dumping of motor vehicles or other things on the highway or elsewhere in the open.

The deposit of poisonous, noxious or polluting waste in circumstances where it could give rise to an environmental hazard was made an offence by the Deposit of Poisonous Waste Act 1972 but this Act was replaced by the major legislation on the topic – the Control of Pollution Act 1974. It is an extensive Act which covers waste on land, pollution of water, noise and pollution of the atmosphere. It defines 'controlled waste' as:

(*a*) household waste – from private dwellings, residential homes, educational institutions, hospitals and nursing homes;

(*b*) industrial waste – from factories, certain nationalised industries other than mines or quarries; and

(*c*) commercial waste – from premises used for trade, business, sport, recreation or entertainment.

The Act makes it an offence for any person, except under licence, to deposit controlled waste on land, or to use any plant or equipment for the purpose of disposing of it. By section 3(2) the person guilty of an offence under the Act can be fined up to £400 on summary conviction, or if convicted on indictment may be imprisoned for up to two years, or fined, or both. Where the waste in question is poisonous, noxious or polluting and likely to cause environmental hazard the maximum term of imprisonment is five years.

Noise on Construction Sites

The Control of Pollution Act 1974 contains provisions relating to noise on construction sites. Where a person intends to carry out works to which section 60 of the Act applies he may make application to the local authority for consent to carry out the work, specifying the works, the methods to be used in undertaking them, and the steps to be taken to minimise the noise resulting from the works. The consent forthcoming may include conditions to be fulfilled, or may be limited or qualified to allow for any change in circumstances. A time limit may also be placed on the consent.

If the local authority fails to give a consent within twenty-eight days of receipt of the application the applicant has a further twenty-one days within which to appeal to the magistrates' court. The same situation applies where the consent is given, but is conditional, qualified or limited in any way.

If no prior consent has been sought by the developer and it appears to the local authority that the works are being, or are going to be carried out, and are of the kind caught by section 60, the authority may serve a notice imposing requirements such as a specification of plant or machinery which may or may not be used, the time limits within which the works may be carried out, the level of noise which may be emitted, and it may also make provision for a change in circumstances. The local authority must have due regard to codes of practice issued under the Act and to the need for ensuring that the best practicable means are used to cut down the noise levels. Before specifying particular methods or plant or machinery the authority should draw to the attention of the recipient other plant or machinery which would be substantially as effective in minimising noise and would be more acceptable to the local authority, and to the need to protect persons in the locality from the effects of noise.

But what works are caught by the Act? By section 60 (1) the Act has application to:

(a) the erection, construction, alteration, repair or maintenance of buildings, structures or roads;

(b) breaking up, opening or boring under any road or adjacent land in connection with the construction, inspection, maintenance or removal of works;

(c) demolition or dredging work; and

(d) work of engineering construction.

The notice is served on the person who appears to be carrying out or about to carry out the works in question, and on such others who appear to be responsible for, or to have control over, the carrying out of the works.

Once the notice is served, a person who contravenes a requirement of the notice he has received is guilty of an offence. If he has received a consent from the authority a notice would not normally be forthcoming; but such a consent does not necessarily absolve him from liability under the Act. Where, for instance, he has received a consent but has not taken all reasonable steps to bring the consent to the notice of the person who is actually carrying out the works, a contravention of the requirements of the consent will lead to a possible charge of an offence under section 60(8).

Thermal Insulation

By the Thermal Insulation (Industrial Buildings) Act 1957 new factories and existing extensions to existing factories must be insulated against loss of heat. Local authorities must take this into account when studying plans deposited for approval under the building regulations; if the plans show the buildings will not conform to the standard laid down in the Act they must be rejected. The Secretary for Trade and Industry may make regulations restricting the use of certain materials in insulation; plans not conforming to these regulations must be rejected unless the materials are to be used in such a way as not to enhance the risk of fire. Whole classes of buildings are exempted by the regulations, however, and on grounds of expediency local authorities may exempt particular buildings with the consent of the Secretary of State.

If a building is constructed in contravention of the Act the local authority may require its demolition and if the owner fails to comply with the notice the authority may demolish or alter the building and charge the cost to the owner. This local authority action must be taken, however, within twelve months of the completion of the building. Disputes between an owner and the local authority may be settled by the Secretary of State.

Fire Safety

In addition to the above precautions an obligation is placed upon local authorities to ensure that theatres, halls, or other buildings used as places of public resort, and restaurants, shops or warehouses to which the public is admitted, and in which more than twenty people are employed, must have satisfactory means of ingress and egress. If the authority is dissatisfied it may serve notice on the owner to take steps to rectify the matter; if the authority considers immediate action is necessary it may apply to the magistrates for a temporary closing order: section 59, Public Health Act 1936. This control does not apply where the premises have a current fire certificate under the Offices, Shops and Railway Premises Act 1963.

By section 16 of the Housing Act 1961 local authorities can require adequate means of escape in case of fire in houses in multiple occupation. In other cases, where buildings are more than two storeys high and an upper storey is more than twenty feet from the ground, the authorities are under an obligation to require the provision of adequate means of escape in case of fire where the buildings in question:

(*a*) are let in flats or tenements; or

(*b*) are used as hotels, hospitals or other institutions; or

(*c*) are used as restaurants, shops, stores or warehouses and have sleeping accommodation for employees on any upper floor (unless a fire certificate under the Offices, Shops and Railway Premises Act 1963 is currently in force).

Sanitation Provisions

A general duty lies upon local authorities to provide sewers and disposal works for the treatment and disposal of sewage. The Public Health Act 1875 vested all sewers in local authorities, but drains remained within private ownership. This led to difficulties of definition since 'drains' were regarded as pipes leading to one house only; otherwise, they were 'sewers'. Thus, in *Hill v. Aldershot Corporation* (1933) it could be said:[4]

'Once you get the drainage of two buildings, whether occupied by the same or different persons, into a drain, it becomes a sewer repairable by the local authority, though it is on private land, and though no one else can drain into it without the authority of the owner of the land.'

Reform was not properly carried out until the Public Health Act 1936 introduced new and simpler rules for sewers constructed after 1936, with the distinction drawn between 'public' sewers (vested in the local authority) and 'private' sewers.

Definitions of Sewers and Drains. Section 343 defined the relevant terms as follows:

- (*a*) a drain is a pipe used to drain one building, or buildings or yards of buildings within the same curtilage;
- (*b*) a sewer is a pipe used to drain buildings or yards of buildings not within the same curtilage.

Responsibility for the maintenance of drains is private; responsibility for sewers differs according to whether they are *public* sewers or *private* sewers.

It is the duty of the water authorities to maintain, cleanse and empty public sewers, but they can recover the cost of the repair, renewal and improvement of lengths of public sewer from the owners of land through which those lengths pass:

- (i) where the sewer is one which before 1937 was repairable by persons other than the local authority; or
- (ii) where the sewer lies in a garden, court or yard, or a private street used mainly for access to premises in it, and was not constructed by the authority.

Where several owners are involved, the cost may be apportioned among them, with the authority taking into account the relative benefit enjoyed by each and the responsibility for the act which made the work essential.

But what are public sewers? Section 20 of the Public Health Act 1936 defines them as those constructed:

- (*a*) before 1 October, 1937;[5]
- (*b*) by the local authority and not draining only property belonging to the authority;

(c) under a private street works procedure, to the authority's satisfaction; or

(d) after 1 October, 1937 and adopted as public sewers by a declaration of vesting.

Sewers which do not fall within these definitions are classified as private sewers.

Provision of Public Sewers. By section 14 of the Water Act 1973 a water authority is under a duty to provide such public sewers as may be necessary for the effectual draining of its area, though in certain cases it can claim contributions for the cost of constructing a public sewer from frontagers. Where the authority is in default an aggrieved person can lodge a complaint with the Secretary of State for the Environment but no action for mandamus can lie. The remedy, it was pointed out in *Robinson v. Workington Corporation* (1897), was provided in the statute: a complaint to the local government board, and this was upheld in *Smeaton v. Ilford Corporation* (1954). The *Smeaton* case nevertheless underlined the fact that while inaction could give rise to no remedy other than a complaint to the Secretary of State (the Local Government Board, previously) an authority which undertakes its duties negligently or improperly can be sued for damages. Because the sewer was overloaded Smeaton was caused inconvenience by the erupting sewage and he sued in nuisance. The situation had arisen because owners of newly built houses in the area had exercised their right to have their drains connected to the sewer. The authority had not been *negligent*, and had not therefore *created* the nuisance. Section 31 of the Public Health Act 1936 obliged the authority to discharge its functions so as not to create a nuisance and so excluded liability in the absence of negligence; in the event Smeaton was unable to succeed in his claim, but the judgment emphasised that, if positive action had created the nuisance, liability on the part of the authority could follow.

In carrying out its duty to provide public sewers a water authority may build public sewers in streets, after due notice, and through private land after giving reasonable notice to the owner and occupier. Compensation may be payable where the sewer runs through private land.

Section 14 of the Water Act 1973 also states that a private developer who intends to build a drain or sewer may be required by the authority to construct it as part of the general system of drainage, but any additional cost thus incurred must then be met by the authority.

Owners and occupiers of land are entitled, on giving notice to the water authority, to have their drains or sewers drained into public sewers – although special provisions apply in the case of trade effluents (see below, p. 74). The authority may refuse permission only if the construction or condition of the pipe would detrimentally affect the sewerage system.

Subject to certain conditions owners and occupiers may require the water authority to provide a public sewer for *domestic* purposes. The conditions are that the water authority can secure that the charges reasonably incurred or any reasonable deficit will be met by the owners or occupiers in question. By section 16 of the Water Act 1973 failure to provide a public sewer within six months can lead to the water authority being penalised, unless it can show that the failure was due to unavoidable accident, or other unavoidable cause. The six-month period may be extended by agreement. Disputes are determined by a referee.

The functions of the water authority may be discharged through the agency of the local authorities (district councils and London boroughs), who may carry out the programme approved by the water authority, with expenses met by the water authority. Sewage disposal, trade effluent control and the maintenance and operation of sewers vested before 1 April 1974 in joint sewerage boards or the Greater London Council are expressly excluded from these agency arrangements.

Quite apart from such agencies the water authority must consult the local authority before it builds, diverts or closes a public sewer, and when the work is done it must inform the local authority. On the other hand, local authorities also have a duty to notify the water authority of proposals brought to their notice for the erection or extension of a building over a public sewer – and in such cases the water authority may give directions to the local authority in the exercise of the local authority's functions in this matter.

Trade Effluents. The right to connect with a public sewer is limited, as has already been pointed out, where trade effluents are concerned. Special rules relate to the discharge of trade effluent (liquid, with or without suspended particles, produced in the course of trade or industry) whereby the water authority's consent to discharge must be obtained in all except certain privileged instances. This right to discharge applies to cases where effluent of the same nature and composition was discharged prior to the Public Health (Drainage of

Trade Premises) Act 1937 but sections 55 to 57 of the Public Health Act 1961 allows water authorities to demand charges and impose certain conditions with regard to these discharges. Where a firm fails to exercise its right to discharge for two years the right lapses.

In all other cases the consent of the water authority is necessary before trade effluents can be discharged into public sewers. A trade effluent notice must be served on the authority, which may consent unconditionally, or consent subject to limitations and conditions which may be varied from time to time. The authority may also direct that no discharge shall take place before a specified date. Additionally, an offence is committed under section 32 of the Control of Pollution Act 1974 if trade effluent or sewage effluent is discharged into rivers and 'controlled waters' (see below, p. 82) unless a disposal licence is obtained, or unless a 'consent' can be shown, or a licence under the Dumping at Sea Act 1974, or some other statutory authority shown, or certain other accepted practices relied on.

Sewage Disposal. The water authorities are under a duty to deal effectually with sewerage by means of sewage disposal works or otherwise. Before the sewage is discharged into streams or rivers it must be purified so that the quality of the stream or river into which it is discharged is not prejudicially affected. If the water authority finds that polluting matter has been discharged it can take proceedings against the offender in a court of summary jurisdiction; other persons may bring an action with the consent of the Attorney-General. Before such proceedings can be instituted a month must elapse after service of a notice to the offender that proceedings are under consideration.

If it is the authority itself which has caused the pollution civil proceedings might lie at the instance of the injured party. Alternatively, the Attorney-General or the injured party may ask for the authority to be restrained from committing or continuing the wrongful act. In *Pride of Derby and Derbyshire Angling Association v. British Celanese* (1953) the defendants had discharged insufficiently treated sewage into the river and Lord Denning said:[6] 'When the increased sewage came in their sewage disposal works . . . they took it under their charge, treated it in their works, and poured the effluent into the River Derwent . . . Their act in pouring a polluting effluent into the river makes them guilty of nuisance.' The Derby Corporation had argued that the sewerage system had been adequate when built, and that it was the increased population of Derby which had really caused the system to become ineffective. The court held there had been an act of misfeasance sufficient to make the corporation liable.

As part of their duties the water authorities must also ensure that drainage is effective and adequate. Where plans are submitted under building regulations the local authority must reject them if the drainage is inadequate, unless it is satisfied that the requirement can be dispensed with. The authority cannot insist that a drain be connected to a sewer unless the public sewer is within 30 metres of the building and the land between is land through which the developer is entitled to take a drain. The position is otherwise where the local authority is prepared to pay the extra cost incurred.

The local authority can require the owner or occupier to carry out remedial works where:

(*a*) an existing building has no satisfactory drainage system; or

(*b*) a drain or private sewer is insufficient or defective or prejudicial to health or a nuisance;

but it cannot require connection to a public sewer more than 30 metres away unless it pays the extra cost involved: section 39, Public Health Act 1936.

If a drain or private sewer is not maintained properly or kept in good repair, where the authority considers the repair can be done for an expenditure of not more than £50 it may, after due notice, undertake the work and recover the cost. If the expenses do not exceed £2, the authority may remit the charge. By section 18 of the Public Health Act, 1961, the court can enquire, in proceedings to recover expenses, into the merits of the notice and as to whether an apportionment of the expenses was fairly made.

Where plans are submitted under building regulations but they show that sanitary accommodation is insufficient and unsatisfactory the authority must reject them. If existing buildings have insufficient or defective sanitary accommodation the authority can serve a notice on the owner requiring remedial work to be carried out (sections 44 and 45, Public Health Act 1936). In appropriate circumstances the authority can require the installation of water closets, and if sanitary accommodation is believed to be defective the authority may excavate for testing purposes, reinstating the land and making good any damage if the apparatus is in order: section 48, Public Health Act 1936.

STATUTORY NUISANCES AND NUISANCE AT COMMON LAW

In *Betts v. Penge Urban District Council* (1942) the tenant of a flat failed to leave under a notice to quit so in an attempt to encourage him to go the landlord removed the door and the window sashes. The local authority intervened, on an interpretation of section 92 of the Public Health Act 1936 which placed the local authority under an obligation to take steps to abate the nuisance arising where premises are in such a state as to be prejudicial to health or a nuisance. The court held that the authority was right in so acting. Lord Caldecote C.J. said:[7]

> If a thing is an interference with the comfort of persons it will be a nuisance. Section 92 goes a little further, and makes it a statutory nuisance, so as to be capable of being remedied in a particular way as provided for in Part III of the Act.

How far in fact does section 92 go? Section 91 of the Act places an obligation upon local authorities to cause inspections to be made of their areas to detect 'statutory nuisances' and to abate them. Five examples of such nuisances are provided in section 92; others are given in other sections of the Act, and in certain other Acts. They are as follows:

(1) Premises kept in such a state as to be prejudicial to health or a nuisance. This was considered in the *Betts* case. In *Springett v. Harold* (1954) it was held that the mere want of internal decorative repair in a dwelling-house would not be a statutory nuisance even if it caused discomfort and inconvenience.

(2) An animal kept in such a place or manner as to be prejudicial to health or a nuisance.

(3) An accumulation or deposit which is prejudicial to health or a nuisance. It is a defence to this charge to show that the accumulation or deposit is necessary for the carrying on of a business and that all precautions have been taken. It does not cover builders' rubble which includes no putrescible matter; such inert matter, if left to accumulate, does not fall under section 92: *Coventry City Council v. Cartwright* (1975).

(4) Dust or effluvia (including spent or ejected steam: section 72, Public Health Act 1961) caused by trade, business, manufacture or process which is prejudicial to the health of or a nuisance to the inhabitants of the neighbourhood. It is a good defence to this charge that the best practicable preventive measures have been taken.

(5) An insufficiently ventilated workplace, or one which is not kept clean or free from noxious effluvia, or which is so overcrowded while work is carried on there as to be prejudicial to the health of employees working there.

(6) A storage container for water used for domestic purposes which is so made or kept as to render the water liable to contamination and to be prejudicial to health (section 94).

(7) A fouled watercourse or one that is choked or silted so as to be prejudicial to health or a nuisance (section 259(1)).

(8) A tent, van, shed or similar structure so overcrowded or deficient in sanitary accommodation as to be prejudicial to health or a nuisance (section 268(2)).

(9) The emission of smoke in certain defined circumstances (sections 16 to 45, Clean Air Act 1956).

Where an authority is satisfied that a statutory nuisance exists it may serve upon the person by whose act, default or sufferance the nuisance arises or continues, an abatement notice. If the person responsible cannot be found the notice may be served on the owner or occupier of the premises on which the nuisance arises. The abatement notice served under section 91 of the Public Health Act 1936 will also state what needs to be done to put the matter right. If the nuisance arises from a structural defect the notice must be served on the owner of the premises, but if the person responsible cannot be found and the owner or occupier is blameless the authority may itself abate the nuisance.

If the nuisance is likely to recur a prohibition notice under the Public Health (Recurring Nuisances) Act 1969 may be served, which may state the works required to prevent the recurrence. In *Peaty v. Field* (1971) it was held that an authority does not need to wait until the nuisance actually recurs before authorising a complaint; it is enough that the nuisance is *likely* to recur. A prohibition notice and an abatement notice can be contained in the same document.

While it normally falls to local authorities to take action upon statutory nuisances there is express provision in the Public Health Act 1936 for private individuals to act. By section 99 of the Act any person who is 'aggrieved' by the existence of a statutory nuisance can complain about it to a justice of the peace. Provided a *prima facie* case is made out he must then issue a summons. The complaint can then be dealt with by the court in the same way as a complaint by a local authority.

Further, under section 99 the court can direct the local authority to abate the nuisance even if they are not the owners of the property – the result is that a quick remedy is provided since there is no need to go through the process of serving an abatement notice, which the authority will have to do. There is another important result for the private individual, however: in *R. v. Epping (Waltham Abbey) Justices, ex*

p. *Birinson* (1948) it was held that under section 99 the local authority itself can be summoned as the landlord, if the authority is responsible for causing the nuisance.

Section 99 has come more into prominence of recent years through its use by tenants' groups to attempt to improve housing conditions in local authority houses. In *Nottingham Corporation v. Newton* (1974) the court held that once a statutory nuisance is proved to the magistrates the section 99 phrase 'the courts shall make an order' means that they *must* make a nuisance order which, by section 94(2), can require the defendant to abate the nuisance by carrying out works, but if the building is not fit for human habitation the court may prohibit its use as a dwelling until the unfitness is cured. The court also said that magistrates could make an order requiring work to be done in phases and might have regard, among other things, to action being taken under the Housing Acts which might result in the property being demolished.

Prohibition notices and abatement notices remain, however, as the general controls exercised by local authorities.

Failure to Comply with Notices. The position here has already been touched upon in the discussion above.

Where the person served with the notice fails to comply with it the authority can apply to a court of summary jurisdiction for a nuisance order. This will call upon the defendant to comply with the notice, and additionally the court may fine the defendant up to £20. It may also prohibit the use of the dwelling-house in question where it considers that the nuisance justifies such an order.

Failure to comply with a nuisance order can lead to the court fining the offender up to £50, with a further penalty of up to £5 per day while the offence continues – and in *Saddleworth Urban District Council v. Aggregate and Sand* (1970) it was held that mere lack of finance does not constitute a good defence in such cases. It is open to the authority to do the work in the event of default and charge the expenses to the person responsible for the nuisance.

By section 26 of the Public Health Act 1961 a swifter procedure for abatement was introduced. In some cases, where premises are regarded as being prejudicial to health or a nuisance and unreasonable delay would follow if the 1936 Act procedure were followed, the authority can serve a notice stating the defects and what it intends to do. Unless the recipient serves a counter-notice within seven days the authority may, within nine days, undertake the necessary work and recover the cost. If a counter-notice is served the authority can proceed only if the work is not begun within a reasonable time, or if reasonable progress has not been made after the work has started.

By section 100 of the 1936 Act, if the authority considers that prosecution in the magistrates' court constitutes an inadequate remedy it may commence proceedings in the High Court for the abatement or prohibition of the nuisance.

Common Law Nuisance

Apart from the statutory nuisances which have been established in the field of public health the common law on nuisance also has an important part to play, as it does generally in other fields such as the law relating to highways.

At common law an unlawful interference may give rise to a civil action for damages or for an injunction or both. A distinction must be drawn between public and private nuisance. The former is a civil wrong – considered here. A public, or common, nuisance is a criminal offence, an act or omission which materially affects the reasonable comfort and convenience of life of a class of the subjects of Her Majesty. Examples of public nuisance are: obstructing a highway or making it dangerous for traffic, keeping a disorderly house or selling unwholesome provisions. In practice many of the instances have been overtaken by statutory provisions.

Private nuisances are themselves of two kinds:

(*a*) a wrongful disturbance of an easement or other servitude appurtenant to land;

(*b*) the act of wrongfully causing or allowing the escape of deleterious things into another person's land: water, smoke, smell, fumes, gas, noise,[8] heat, vibrations,[8] electricity, animals, vegetation, bacteria will suffice as examples.

The private nuisance is actionable only at the suit of the person who is in possession of the land injuriously affected by it. No action will lie unless actual damage can be shown and if the suit is based upon discomfort or inconvenience it must be shown to be substantial – the maxim *de minimis non curat lex* applies. The standard is determined also by the locality where the nuisance is created – 'What would be a nuisance in Belgrave Square would not necessarily be so in Bermondsey'[9] – but in *Hammersmith Railway Co. v. Brand* (1869) where the plaintiff showed that his shrubs and trees had been damaged by

fumes from the defendant's smelting works the plea that the locality
was devoted to works of this kind failed as a defence. It is no defence
that the plaintiff came to the nuisance, nor that the act, although
injurious to the individual, is beneficial to the public at large. Nor is it a
defence to show that the locality is a suitable one for the kind of
business complained of, and negligence is not relevant, any more than
is the claim that others are contributing to the nuisance, or that it
amounts to a reasonable use of the property.

Important though it still remains, the common law has in many
instances been replaced by statutory provisions as has already been
pointed out. The 'statutory nuisances' are examples. Another is
provided by section 107 of the Public Health Act 1936 which lists
certain trades as 'offensive trades' – blood-boiling, fat-extracting
glue-making among them – and states that a person who establishes
such a trade may be fined up to £50 if he does not first obtain the
consent of the local authority. Again, the statement of Farwell J. in
Nicholls v. Ely Beet Sugar Factory (1931) that a pollution action was a
'nuisance action of a kind peculiar to itself' has now received statutory
recognition with the enactment of legislation in 1974 designed to cover
a whole range of activity and replace wholly or in part various other
statutory provisions formerly dealing with some of the problems – such
as the Noise Abatement Act 1960 and the Rivers (Prevention of
Pollution) Act 1951.

THE CONTROL OF POLLUTION ACT 1974

The Act deals with waste on land, pollution of water, noise, and
pollution of the atmosphere.

Disposal of Waste

Part I of the Act deals with disposal of waste on land. 'Waste' is
defined to include any substance which constitutes scrap material,
effluent, or other unwanted surplus arising from the application of any
process, and any substance or article which requires to be disposed of as
being broken, worn out, contaminated or otherwise spoiled (section 30).

The Act itself is largely concerned with 'controlled waste' –
household industrial or commercial waste, and makes it an offence for
any person to deposit controlled waste on land or to use any plant or
equipment to dispose of it, unless licensed to do so. The licensing
authorities are the 'disposal authorities' (county councils, district

councils in Wales, and the Greater London Council). They are under a duty to ensure that adequate arrangements are made for the disposal of controlled waste in their areas and must carry out investigations, in consultation with water authorities, collection authorities (London borough or district councils) and other interested parties. Waste-disposal plans relating to the kinds and quantities of waste to be disposed of in their areas, the methods by which it should be disposed of or reclaimed, the sites and equipment which will be required and the costs involved must be prepared.

By section 12 of the Act it is the duty of the collection authorities to collect without charge all household waste unless it is situated in an isolated or inaccessible place where the cost of collection would be unreasonably high. If the authority is satisfied that adequate arrangements as to collection and disposal are made in such circumstances by the 'controller' of the waste it need not collect. As far as commercial waste is concerned the authority will collect for disposal if requested by the occupier of the premises; in this case, as in that of industrial waste, reasonable charges may be recovered for the service from the person requesting collection.

Section 12(6) empowers the disposal authorities and the collection authorities to carry out necessary construction works for pipes and associated works to collect waste.

The collection authorities must deliver all waste (except paper, which they may decide to retain) to the disposal authorities, or arrange with them for it to be processed for reclamation. The disposal authorities must arrange for the disposal of waste and may provide the necessary sites and equipment and deal with anything produced out of the waste. They may also permit other persons to use their facilities, for which, except in the case of household waste, a proper charge must be made.

The disposal authorities are also the licensing authorities, for the purpose of licensing persons to deposit waste. Sections 3 to 11 of the Act are concerned with licensing matters, in particular matters pertaining to applications for licences, variations of conditions and revocation of licences, their transfer and relinquishment and the supervision of licensed activities. The disposal authorities are bound by section 6(4) to maintain a register of licences which must be kept open to inspection by the public.

The Act also deals with the provision of dustbins and similar receptacles for household waste. These may be provided free of charge by the collection authorities. Receptacles for other waste may be provided on request, but a reasonable charge for this service must normally be made.

Pollution of Water

Part II of the Act is concerned with pollution of water and effectively enlarges the scope of the law previously relating to this matter. The Act brought under control practically all English waters, namely:

(a) controlled waters – coastal waters within three miles of the low-tide line;

(b) restricted waters – tidal rivers and other areas where moorings are commonly provided; and

(c) streams – including rivers, watercourses and inland waters, whether natural or artificial or above or below ground.

Section 31 of the Act makes it an offence to permit the discharge or entry of any poisonous, noxious or polluting matter into such water, or any matter to enter a stream if it may tend, either by itself or in combination with other matter, to impede the flow of water in such a way that pollution due to other causes, or the consequences of such pollution, may be aggravated. It is also an offence to permit any solid waste matter to enter a stream or restricted waters.

There are some circumstances in which pollution may be permitted; these are detailed by section 31 (2). Thus, no offence is committed if the entry is made:

(i) under a disposal licence or consent given under the Act;

(ii) under some other statutory authority, such as section 34 of the Water Act 1945; or local Act or statutory order;

(iii) under a licence granted under the Dumping at Sea Act 1974;

(iv) in accordance with good agricultural practice (unless banned on the ground that water has been or is likely to be polluted);

(v) in an emergency in order to avoid danger to the public;

(vi) by deposit (in certain circumstances) of solid refuse from a mine or quarry.

No offence is committed, similarly, if water from an abandoned mine is permitted to enter relevant waters, or if trade or sewage effluent is permitted to enter other than from a vessel (under section 31(1) (a), (b) and (c).

Additional regulations may be made as to the precautions which may be taken to prevent poisonous, noxious or polluting matter from entering water, and for restricting activities which may give rise to pollution in particular areas, and the Act also provides for by-laws to be made to restrict such activities as putting litter into streams.

Section 32 deals with the matter of trade and sewage effluents. It makes it an offence to discharge such matter into any waters governed by the Act or through a pipe into waters outside the three-mile limit except by a consent or a licence under the Dumping at Sea Act 1974, or from a vessel, or in an emergency to avoid danger to the public. Water authorities may be exempt if they show that the discharge was attributable to a discharge by another person into the sewer or works and the authority was bound to receive it subject to conditions which were not observed (or otherwise was not bound to receive it), and the discharge in question could not reasonably have been expected by the authority.

As far as vessels are concerned, water authorities may make by-laws to prohibit the use of sanitary appliances designed to permit polluting matter to pass into the water on vessels in prescribed areas, and they may ban vessels from streams if the by-laws are not complied with. By section 33(1) such appliances are banned after 1978. Where they are banned the water authorities must provide facilities for the disposal of waste from the vessels concerned.

The water authorities can give 'consents' to discharge polluting matter and these consents may impose conditions relating to the place of discharge and the design of the outlet; the nature, composition, temperature, volume and rate of the discharges; the taking of samples and testing, inspecting, measuring and recording the discharge; the keeping of records and returns; and as to the steps to be taken for preventing the discharges from coming into contact with specified underground water. Detailed procedures for applying for consents are made in the Act, which also deals with revocations and variations. Details of applications must be published unless exempted by the Secretary of State on the ground that publication would prejudice some private interest by disclosing information about a trade secret, or would be contrary to the public interest.

Noise

Part III of the Act deals with noise, including vibration, and imposes a duty on the local authorities to inspect their areas from time to time so as to detect any noise which may amount to a nuisance and to decide how to exercise their powers concerning noise-abatement zones.

By section 58, where an authority considers that noise amounting to a nuisance exists or is likely to occur or recur it can serve on the person responsible (or the owner or occupier of the premises in question if he cannot be found) a notice requiring the nuisance to be abated, or the execution of such works as may be specified in the notice. If the notice is not complied with an offence is committed. It is also open to the local authority to apply to the High Court for an order to abate, restrict or prohibit the nuisance. The occupier of premises may also apply to the magistrates to complain of a nuisance and the court may order its abatement, restriction or prohibition. In such cases, if the order is not complied with the court may direct the local authority to take steps for enforcement of the order.

Defences are available to such complaints, particularly under sections 60 to 66 of the Act which deal with noise arising from construction sites. Where works are being or are about to be carried out on construction sites the local authority may serve a notice imposing requirements as to the way in which they should be carried out, and where work is thus carried out no complaint can then be successful. A person about to carry out work defined in section 60(1) (see page 69 above) can apply for a prior consent.

The Act also deals with noise in streets and repeats provisions formerly contained in the Noise Abatement Act 1960 relating to the use of loudspeakers in streets.

Section 63 deals with the designation of noise-abatement zones, which are areas designated by a local authority by an order confirmed by the Secretary of State. In such zones the authorities must measure the level of noise emanating from premises therein and record the measurements in a noise-level register which must be open to inspection by the public. The level of noise which is registered in respect of any premises must not thereafter be exceeded except by consent of the authority and if the authority considers that the noise emanating from any premises is not acceptable it may serve a notice requiring the noise level to be reduced.

Section 67 covers the question of noise arising from the construction of new buildings. Where it appears to the local authority that a building is going to be constructed and that a noise-abatement order will apply to it when it is erected, or that the premises will be of the kind to which such an order applies, the local authority may determine the noise level on the application of an interested party. The noise level will be recorded and to exceed it thereafter will be an offence. By section 68 provision may also be made by regulations for the purpose of reducing noise caused by plant and machinery. The making of the regulations is the duty of the Secretary of State.

Pollution of the Atmosphere

The prevention of atmospheric pollution is dealt with by Part IV of the Act. The Secretary of State is given power to make regulations relating to the composition and content of fuel for use in motor vehicles and to the sulphur content of oil fuel for use in furnaces and engines. Before making the regulations the Secretary of State must consult representative bodies of vehicle manufacturers and of producers and users of fuel, and experts in air pollution.

By section 79 local authorities are empowered to undertake or contribute towards the cost of research into air pollution and for publicity of information on the subject. They may obtain information about the emission of pollutants:

(*a*) by issuing notices to require occupiers of premises to provide estimates or other information concerning the emission of pollutants;

(*b*) by measuring and recording emissions, through the use of inspectors who may enter premises with or without the agreement of the occupiers; and

(*c*) by entering into arrangements with occupiers whereby the occupiers will measure and record emissions on behalf of the local authority.

With regard to (*b*) above, the authority must give proper notice under section 79 of the Act before acting, and by section 79(5) it must ensure that material published is presented in such a way that no information relating to a trade secret is disclosed except with the consent of the person authorised to disclose it, or with the consent of the Secretary of State.

OTHER GENERAL DUTIES RESPECTING HEALTH

Apart from the powers and duties already mentioned there are a number of other duties exercised by local authorities in respect of health. The Public Health Acts place upon the local authorities the duty to register common lodging houses in its area; provide mortuaries if required to do so by the Secretary of State for the Environment; and exercise supervision over the prevention of infectious disease and food poisoning. Premises in which filling materials are used must be registered with the local authority under the Rag Flock and Other Filling Materials Act 1951, and the Prevention of Damage by Pests Act 1949 places a duty on local authorities to take appropriate steps to ensure as far as is practicable that the area is free from mice and rats. Nursing homes in the local authority area must be registered and the authority has powers of inspection and may make by-laws respecting nursing homes.

Part I of the Caravan Sites and Control of Development Act 1960 introduced a licensing system to regulate the establishment and operation of caravan sites, and enabled local authorities to provide and operate them if they so wished. Conditions may be attached to the licences. By section 269 of the Public Health Act 1936 it is an offence for a person to keep a moveable dwelling (other than a caravan) on any site for more than forty-two consecutive days or sixty days in any twelve consecutive months unless a licence is obtained from the local authority, though the Secretary of State for the Environment may grant general exemption from this provision to a recognised camping or other organisation. By section 268 by-laws may be made with respect to tents, vans, sheds and similar structures used for human habitation and where such structures are overcrowded or insufficiently provided with sanitary accommodation, or for some other reason are prejudicial to health or a nuisance a 'statutory nuisance' exists and may be dealt with as such.

Other powers and duties relating to health generally may be found in the Food and Drugs Act 1955, the Trade Descriptions Act 1968, Offices, Shops and Railway Premises Act 1963, Health and Safety at Work Act 1974 and Fire Precautions Act 1971.

REFERENCES

1. Together with the other legislation noted.
2. 'Rubbish' does not here mean material accumulated in the course of business, or 'waste' deposited under a disposal licence.
3. Under Class I of Schedule 1, Class II of Schedule 1 and Classes IV.I, VI.I and VIII.I of Schedule 1 respectively.
4. [1933] 1 K.B. 259.
5. Except those constructed for profit (a benefit other than the removal of sewage).
6. [1953] Ch. 149, p. 191.
7. [1942] 2 K.B. 154, p. 159.
8. See now the Control of Pollution Act 1974.
9. *Sturges v. Bridgman* (1879), 11 Ch.D., per Thesiger L.J., p. 865.

5

Law of Highways

Statute law on highways dates back to the sixteenth century and the Public Health Act 1875 contained provisions to ensure that streets were arranged and constructed in such a way as to further healthy conditions. Much of the statute law was consolidated in the Highways Act 1959, which repealed many redundant and obsolete provisions. The 1959 Act remains the principal legislation, amended by the Highways (Miscellaneous Provisions) Act 1961, the Public Health Act 1961 (Part IV) and the Highways Act 1971.

A highway is a defined strip of land over which the public has the right to pass and re-pass. It need not amount to a thoroughfare since a cul-de-sac can be a highway, but the right of passage may be limited: highways are commonly created by 'dedication' and the dedicator may limit the extent of the right of passage.

CREATION OF HIGHWAYS

Although dedication and acceptance is a common method of creation for highways it is not the only one; highways may also be created by statute.

Dedication and Acceptance

Dedication – whereby a landowner dedicates a right of passage across his land for the use of the public at large – may be express or implied, but there must be, in any case, an *intention* to dedicate. Normally the intention will be seen in a formal document, but in the case of implied dedications the act of the owner must conclusively point to the intention to dedicate. To *permit* passage is one thing; dedication is another.

The dedication will be ineffective, in addition, if it restricts the right of user to particular groups or classes of people. It may limit the *mode* of user, but it must be open to members of the public in general. Furthermore, to dedicate effectively the dedicator must have the power to dedicate – he must be capable of giving a grant over his land for all time. Thus, generally, it is only the owner of land in fee simple who can make an effective dedication.

Mere dedication as such does not create a highway. There must also be an acceptance by the public of the dedication. The acceptance does not require a formal act; acceptance by user is enough, but it must be an acceptance as of right, not on sufferance or by licence. Thus, although 'acceptance by the public is ordinarily proved by user by the public; and user by the public is also evidence of dedication by the owner'[1] the user must be open and unobstructed and as of right. The courts will always look at circumstances as a whole and take into account any evidence which negatives the claim that an intention to dedicate has been shown, as is proved by unobstructed user. At common law there was an inference that if the highway was used over a long period dedication could be presumed, but the Rights of Way Act 1932[2] stated principles upon which assumptions could be presumed to apply. The provisions were later replaced by sections 34 and 35 of the Highways Act 1959[3] and the situation now is as follows.

If a way has been actually enjoyed by the public as of right and without interruption for a full period of twenty years the way is deemed to have been dedicated as a highway. This presumption can be rebutted by evidence to the contrary and an owner can negative the inference by placing an appropriate notice denying the intention to dedicate on the way. If the notice is removed or destroyed he can still protect his rights by giving notice to the county council (or London borough council) that the way has not been dedicated, and he may also submit maps of his land delineating the ways he admits as dedicated. He may subsequently declare that no further ways have been dedicated.

This is a simplification of the earlier procedure applying and the issues in any particular case will be settled by the application of these principles to the evidence adduced. Where public paths are concerned the National Parks and Access to the Countryside Act 1949 placed upon county councils the duty of ascertaining and recording the existence of public paths (footpaths and bridle-ways) and roads used as public paths. A map and statement will contain the council's findings in each area, and these may be subject to review.

It should be emphasised that the statutory provisions did not supersede the common-law rules completely: a claim based on dedication and acceptance under the common law can still succeed if the conditions are fulfilled at common law.

Creation by Statute

There are various ways in which highways can be created by statute. A local Act may sometimes provide for the creation of a highway; they may be created under general powers incorporated in a statute; or they may be created by specific provision such as in the Highways Act 1971.

The Highways Act 1959 enables the local authorities and the Secretary of State to construct highways, provide road ferries and special roads reserved for particular classes of vehicles. The Highways Act 1971 gives the authorities powers to stop up private accesses, close roads, divert watercourses and construct bridges over and tunnels under navigable watercourses – in order to speed up the construction of trunk roads and motorways. Under the 1959 Act the council of a county, district, London borough and a National Park joint planning board may enter a public path agreement to dedicate public paths, with or without limitations and restrictions. The National Parks and Access to the Countryside Act 1949 contains provisions as to the creation of long-distance routes which allow the public to journey on foot or horseback over ways not principally used by vehicles.

HIGHWAY AUTHORITIES

The principal highway authorities are the Secretary of State for the Environment, county councils, the Greater London Council, the London borough councils and the Council of the City of London. They do not, however, exercise *all* the highway functions; some are carried out by district, parish and community councils, and some functions are exercised by district councils as agents of county councils.

The highway authority for trunk roads (the principal roads constituting the national system of routes for through traffic) is the Secretary of State. The trunk roads are listed in the Trunk Roads Acts of 1936 and 1946. By sections 7 and 26 of the 1959 Act the Secretary of State may designate other roads as trunk roads. Though the Secretary of State remains the highway authority for these roads, in practice most of the work is undertaken by county councils as his agents – and they themselves often delegate the work to district councils.

All other roads fall to the county councils as highway authorities (except in London where the Greater London Council is the highway authority for the metropolitan – or principal – roads, and the borough councils and Common Council of the City of London are highway authorities for all roads excluding metropolitan and trunk roads).

Special roads may be the responsibility of any highway authority, as may walk-ways (ways over, through or under buildings or structures); principal roads[4] and classified roads are the responsibility of the county councils.

REPAIRS AND IMPROVEMENTS

By section 214 of the Highways Act 1959, and other statutory provisions, highway authorities have wide powers to purchase land by agreement or under compulsion, to construct and improve highways, even if the land lies outside the boundary of the highway or proposed highway.[5] They can purchase land needed to reduce the adverse effects of the existence or use of the highway on its surroundings, and by section 22 of the Land Compensation Act 1973 can acquire by agreement owner-occupied property which is severely affected by construction works or by the use of a new or improved road, within twelve months.

Where the construction, improvement, existence or use of a highway has, or will have an adverse effect upon the surroundings the highway authority can mitigate those effects by carrying out such works as tree-planting, or the provision of shrubs and plants or the laying out of grass areas. It may acquire land for this purpose; that land can be developed and re-developed to improve the surroundings of the highway. The authority may enter agreements with frontagers which may contain appropriate financial provisions.

These provisions of the Land Compensation Act 1973 do not affect the rights of authorities to acquire under the Highways Act 1971 rights instead of titles, which may be created over land for highway purposes by using compulsory powers. Thus, where an authority wishes to construct and maintain bridges over highways and tunnels under highways, or intends building drains, rather than take title to the land affected it may under section 47 of the 1971 Act acquire rights instead.

Repair Responsibilities of Highway Authorities

Local highway authorities are responsible for the repair of those highways 'maintainable at the public expense'. These include highways existing before 1836 and those highways which have either been adopted under the Highways Act 1835 or have been adopted under other subsequent statutes containing adoption provisions. The principal provisions are found in section 39 of the Highways Act 1959 (which largely re-enacted, with modifications, the 1835 provisions), sections 82 and 152 of the Public Health Act 1875 (relating to private street works), sections 19 and 20 of the Private Street Works Act 1892 and section 6 of the New Streets Act 1951, were also re-enacted in the Highways Act 1959.

An authority may adopt a private street after private street works have been carried out and may be required to make up and adopt a private street where payment has been made under the advance payments code. A person liable to maintain a privately maintainable highway can also have his liability taken over by the highway authority if he pays an appropriate sum. Where such a highway is diverted by order of a magistrates' court the substituted highway becomes the responsibility of the highway authority.

While county councils are responsible for all highways maintainable at public expense (other than trunk roads) as far as maintenance is concerned it is the district council which will have responsibility in respect of footpaths, bridle-ways and urban roads (which are neither trunk roads nor classified roads). The district council first informs the county council of the highways or parts of highways over which it intends to exercise its powers; the county council may issue a counter-notice, and the Secretary of State has power to settle disagreements. But the county councils must in any case reimburse the district councils their expenses in matters of maintenance – other expenses are met by the district council itself.

The highway authorities can improve highways, provide equipment for them and make provision for picnic sites and public conveniences.

Repair Responsibilities of the Secretary of State

The Secretary of State is responsible as a highway authority for the repair of trunk roads but in practice, as the highway authorities delegate the work to district councils, so does the Secretary of State use the county councils to carry out his responsibilities on an agency basis.

Repair Responsibilities of Private Persons

Liability for the repair of highways by private persons can arise in three ways.

(1) Liability may arise by prescription, where a body or person is shown to have carried out repairs 'time out of mind'.

(2) Liability can arise *ratione tenurae*, where it arises as a result of the tenure of particular lands. This will be in the nature of an obligation which will run with the land and is normally proved by showing that the occupier and his predecessors have for many years carried out the works of repair to the highway in question.

(3) Liability can arise *ratione clausurae*, where the right to use open land adjoining a road in order to bypass the road when it becomes impassable has been acquired by the public. It must be shown that the owner has enclosed the open land so that the public can no longer enjoy the right to bypass the road – the owner then becomes liable on account of his enclosure, and must keep the highway in repair.

Highways for which no one is Responsible for Repair

Roads which have come into existence since 1835 and which have not been adopted by the highway authority are known generally as 'private streets'. Ordinary repairs to these streets are the responsibility of no one, though by section 204 of the Highways Act 1959[6] the highway authority may require frontagers to carry out urgent repairs and if they default the authority can undertake the work, recovering the cost thereafter from the owners concerned. By section 47 of the Public Health Act 1961 the authority can undertake work of its own volition to prevent or remove a danger arising out of want of repair, where it is seen as an emergency.

Highway authorities have, in addition, statutory power to call for the making up of private streets. Two sets of procedures (the 'codes' of 1892 and 1875) were available before 1972; the Local Government Act 1972, by section 188 made the 1892 code of general application. Outside Greater London, county councils are the street works authorities; in London the authorities are the London borough councils and the Common Council of the City of London. Under the 1892 code an authority can resolve to pave, sewer and light a private street, prepare plans and specifications for the work, estimate the costs and apportion them, provisionally, among owners of land which fronts, abuts on to or adjoins the private street. The resolution must be published locally and notices served on the owners, with relevant documents deposited at district and county offices. In fixing the apportionment of cost individual benefits from the works may be taken into account, but frontage is the overriding consideration. The authority can make a contribution to the cost and may bring into the apportionment premises which do not abut onto the street. On completion of the works a notice of final apportionment of expenses is served on owners affected. Once made up the road may be declared by the authority to be a highway maintainable at the public expense, but if the owners object it must remain a private street (unless the majority objection is overruled by the magistrates' court).

Provisional apportionments can be appealed against on six grounds detailed in section 177 of the Highways Act 1959; section 180 of the Act details three grounds on which objections to final apportionment can be lodged.

If payment of expenses for private street works is not made an authority can recover the debt with interest in the magistrates' court, or in the county court or the High Court. The expenses become a charge on the premises so the owner of the premises will be liable for the payment.

The advance payments code provides for the payment of sums likely to be required to meet the cost of street works before new buildings are erected in private streets. Under the code payment may be made, or security given for it, to the authority, and frontagers are able to call for the works to be carried out by the local authority and the street adopted when development has reached a certain stage.

The code does not apply where buildings are erected within the curtilage of existing buildings or where the owner has entered an agreement under section 40 of the Highways Act 1959 (under which new roads are built at his expense). Nor does the code apply where the authority is satisfied that the development is isolated, or remote from made-up streets, or where development fills in gaps in a street already substantially built up, or where the frontage is substantially industrial.

Where more than half the frontage is made up in the street and the code provisions applied to at least one building the majority of the frontagers may call on the authority to require the street to be made up and, in due course, adopt it.

Under the Local Government Act 1972 the code applies where it did formerly (to boroughs and urban districts and rural districts but not inner London boroughs) and can be made to apply elsewhere in parishes and communities by resolution of the county council. The approval of the Secretary of State was previously necessary, but this is no longer the case.

The code is given in sections 192 to 199 of the Highways Act 1959 and the Local Government Act 1972, Schedule 21, paras 70, 71 and 72.

Public Paths. Before 1949 public paths were repairable by the inhabitants at large but by section 47 of the National Parks and Access to the Countryside Act 1949 the liability for paths coming into existence after 16 December 1949 fell to the highway authority if they were dedicated to the use of the public under a public path order or agreement. Otherwise no one was under a duty to repair. Though the Act was repealed by the Highways Act 1959 the rules remain, under the 1959 Act.[7]

A duty to maintain bridle-ways and footpaths does, however, fall to district, parish or community councils and by sections 27 to 31 of the Countryside Act 1968 highway authorities must signpost or mark footpaths and bridle-ways wherever they leave a metalled road. Landowners are responsible for stiles repair but one-quarter of the expenses reasonably incurred in maintenance must be paid by the highway authority, which may pay more if it wishes.

Standard of Repair

The rule was laid down as long ago as 1915.[8]

> It is the duty of road authorities to keep their public highways in a state fit to accommodate the ordinary traffic which passes or may be expected to pass along them. As the ordinary traffic expands or changes in character, so must the nature of the maintenance and repair of the highway alter to suit the change.

The person who complains that a highway is out of repair may serve notice on the authority or person liable for maintenance requiring the repair work to be carried out. If the claim is disputed the matter is resolved by the Crown Court. If it is merely the *extent* of repairs required which is in dispute the matter can be settled in the magistrates' court.

The standard of repair may well be important where the issue of liability to a member of the public injured by the want of repair is concerned. Formerly, civil liability arose only in cases of *mal*feasance; non-feasance – that is, doing *nothing* by way of repair – could lead to no liability. The defence of non-feasance was removed by section 1 of the Highways (Miscellaneous Provisions) Act 1961; instead it provided the authorities with a new defence. If an authority could prove that it had taken such care as in the circumstances was all that was reasonably required to make the highway safe for traffic no liability would follow. The court would take into account the character of the highway, the amount of traffic expected to use it, the standard of maintenance appropriate for it, the state in which a reasonable person would expect to find the highway, whether the authority knew or could reasonably be expected to have known that the condition of the highway was likely to cause danger to users, and whether warning notices had been displayed (in those cases where the authority could not reasonably have been expected to have time to carry out repairs before the accident occurred). The standard of repair, and the test to determine it, was put in a nutshell by Cumming-Bruce J. in *Littler v. Liverpool Corporation* (1968):

> The test in relation to a length of pavement is reasonable foreseeability of danger. A length of pavement is only dangerous if, in the ordinary course of human affairs, danger may reasonably be anticipated from its continued use by the public who usually pass over it.[9]

It should be added that the defence of contributory negligence is also available to the highway authority where injury is caused through failure to repair to an appropriate standard.

Precautions in Repair Works

The question of protection of the public using highways has been the subject of much litigation in the courts, and Parliament has also put its mind to the problem. The liability of the highway authority to a member of the public in respect of injuries sustained as a result of failure to repair, or negligent repair, has already been discussed, p. 94 above. But what of injuries sustained while works of repair and improvement are being carried out?

The common-law duty placed upon highway authorities was discussed in *Haley v. London Electricity Board* (1965). The L.E.B. dug a trench in the street. Section 6 of the Public Utilities Street Works Act 1950 obliged them to fence and guard the trench. A workman placed a punner hammer across the payment, its handle on railings two feet high, its end resting on the pavement. It was intended to prevent pedestrians from walking into the excavation but *H* was blind: he missed the hammer with his stick and fell into the trench and was injured. The House of Lords held that the L.E.B. (acting through its workman) had not exercised reasonable care and was therefore liable.

Statutory rules also exist with regard to the precautions which must be taken when repair or improvement works are being undertaken.

Section 148 of the Highways Act 1959 states that barriers must be erected to prevent danger to traffic (which includes pedestrians and animals) and works must be properly guarded and lighted during the hours of darkness. Guarding and fencing requirements are also laid down in section 8 of the Public Utilities Street Works Act 1950, and by section 150 of the Highways Act 1959 a duty is placed on all local authority employees to take reasonable precautions when materials are being placed by them to remain on the highway during the hours of darkness. This is a particularly important provision where building works are being carried out, for such materials may amount to dangerous obstructions. The matter can be dealt with further in a discussion of nuisance and obstructions (see page 98).

RIGHTS IN RESPECT OF HIGHWAYS

The dedication of a highway to the public does not divest the owners of the soil over which the highway passes of their rights of ownership over that soil. Equally, the adjoining owner has a right to use the airspace over the highway, so he may tunnel under or build above, the highway. He also has a right of access to the highway from any part of his premises provided he exercises that right reasonably and without interfering with the reasonable exercise of the public's right of way. But while this is the position at common law, statute has whittled away at these rights in effect.

Section 153 of the Highways Act 1959 states that an adjoining owner may tunnel under the highway only with the consent of the highway authority; by section 152 he must obtain a consent also to place a cable, beam or other apparatus above it. Section 22 of the Town and Country Planning Act 1971 states that consent of the authority is needed for 'development' – and this includes the formation of and laying out of a means of access to a highway; and section 40 of the Highways Act 1971 states that where an occupier of premises habitually crosses a footway with a vehicle the highway authority may ensure that a carriageway is made – at the occupier's expense.

Public rights to use the highway are also limited. The right is to pass and re-pass – though this may include parking a vehicle on the highway while taking a meal. The rule is thus to be construed reasonably, but the rights of adjoining owners were recognised in the classic case of *Harrison v. Duke of Rutland* (1893). *R* owned moorland crossed by highways and *H* used one highway to frighten grouse and spoil the shooting party organised by *R*. He refused to stop his interference and was held down by keepers until the shoot was over. He sued *R* for assault, but the court held that *H* was a trespasser. He was not merely passing and re-passing; he was committing a trespass against the owner of the soil – *R*.[10]

The highways themselves vest in the highway authorities, and this ownership includes as much of the soil of the street as is necessary to preserve and maintain it to the two top spits. Local authorities and statutory undertakers can open streets to lay apparatus such as gas mains only by statutory authority – otherwise, a nuisance is committed. The authority necessary is usually contained in the statute relating to the service provided. The procedure to be followed appears in the Public Utilities Street Works Act 1950. This Act contains two codes.

The Street Works Code. This code, contained in Part I of the Act, details the procedure to be followed where it is proposed to lay apparatus in a street, or undertake work in connection with the apparatus. Details of the work must be given to the highway authority or the persons responsible for the management or control of the street. If the proposal is rejected reference to arbitration must be made. Emergency works require no notification. Notice of commencement of works and supervision of reinstatement works are also covered by the code.

Part II Code. The code in Part II of the Act deals with cases where the highway authority proposes to undertake works which will disturb an undertaker's apparatus, and prescribes the notices required. The cost of protective works must be carried by the highway authority unless they are remedying subsidence for which they are blameless, or the undertakers have placed or renewed apparatus in a road after they have had notice of the authority's works (the notice is effective if the works are commenced within two years after it is given). The authority's liability for costs is also limited where the undertakers use the opportunity to replace apparatus by a better type or to renew apparatus placed in the road more than seven and a half years earlier.

Section 136[11] of the Highways Act 1959 states that statutory undertakers may not open or break up a carriageway during the twelve months following a period during which a road has been closed to vehicular traffic, or the width reduced to less than two-thirds, for the carrying out of roadworks (or roadworks and other works). A similar embargo is placed on the twelve-month period following the completion of resurfacing which extends to one-third or more of the width of the carriageway. The provision has no application to emergency works, or to the situation where the highway authority consents to the works being carried out.

Controlled Land

Controlled land is that land which abuts on a maintainable highway or on one likely to become repairable at public expense, and which is to be used for road purposes because the authority uses it, or has authority to acquire it compulsorily, or has reserved it by prescribing an improvement line under section 72 of the Highways Act 1959. The powers contained in the Public Utilities Street Works Act 1950 have application to controlled land as well as to highways as such.

Street works under the code, or works carried out by highway authorities in general, or by others, including statutory undertakers, are almost bound to cause inconvenience to the public. Additionally, they may give rise to hazards and nuisances. It will be appropriate therefore, at this point, to examine the statutory and common-law rules that apply where nuisance or obstructions might arise as a result of work carried out on the highway.

NUISANCE AND INTERFERENCE WITH THE HIGHWAY

Offences may arise in connection with the use of a highway, or interference with a highway, both at civil and criminal law. In some cases the matter contravenes a statutory provision; in others it may be a common-law offence that has been committed.

Statutory Provisions

The principal statutory provisions relating to highways are found in the Highways Act 1959, which enumerates a number of different forms of interference and obstruction. The wilful obstruction of a highway is dealt with by section 121 – and it was held in *Arrowsmith v. Jenkins* (1963) that *mens rea* was not a constituent part of the offence – it is not necessary to show that the party charged with the offence *intended* to cause an obstruction. Other offences appear in section 117 (causing damage to the highway) and 119 (ploughing up a footpath), but of more relevance to the construction industry are the provisions found in sections 140 and 146 of the Highways Act 1959 and section 71 of the Highways Act 1971.

By section 140 of the 1959 Act where a person deposits without lawful authority anything on a highway and someone using the highway is injured or endangered as a result, the depositor can be fined (not more than £100: Third Schedule, Criminal Justice Act, 1967). The penalty here stated is a general one; special provision is made with regard to the construction industry by section 146, as amended by section 71 of the Highways Act 1971. By these provisions:

(1) A person may, with the consent of the highway authority, temporarily deposit building materials, rubbish and other things in the street, or make a temporary excavation there.

(2) If the highway authority refuses its consent an 'aggrieved' party can appeal to the magistrates' court.

(3) Where materials or rubbish have been placed on the street, or an excavation made there, the obstruction or excavation must be fenced adequately, and during the hours of darkness it must be properly lighted. If the highway authority requires removal of the obstruction or the filling-in of the excavation this must be done, and in any case the obstruction or excavation must not be allowed to remain longer than is necessary.

(4) A person contravening these provisions can be fined up to £10 for every day on which the offence is continued. The local authority also has the power to remove the obstruction or fill in the excavation and recover the expenses reasonably incurred from the person guilty of the offence.

These provisions cover the siting of skips (bins and hoppers) on the highway, and the matter was first tested in *Gatland v. Metropolitan Police Commissioner* (1968) where a driver, employed by George Sands & Co. Ltd, was accused of 'depositing, without lawful authority or excuse, a hopper on the highway, in consequence whereof a user was endangered'. His employers were accused of aiding and abetting him. The Lord Chief Justice concluded that the hopper, parked on a broad, well-lit road, had not constituted a true hazard and the prosecution failed. It follows that if the circumstances as to weather, lighting, or degree of protrusion into the road are different, so as to constitute a hazard, liability could follow. Two cases in point arose in 1972: in *Wills v. T. F. Martin (Roof Contractors) Ltd* (1972) it was held that even if a skip is placed in the road so as to be an obstruction the motorist who hits it *solely* because he did not look where he was going, cannot claim damages from the builder who deposited the skip; in that case the skip was lit, but in *Drury v. Camden London Borough Council* (1972) the skip was unlit during the hours of darkness and the defendant was held liable – though the scooter driver who was injured after colliding with it was also held partly to blame. A third 1972 decision raised the question of the standard of illumination necessary for skips placed in the highway: in *Saper v. Hungate* (1972) it was held that the skip must be lit so as to be instantly visible. Thus, the driver who collided with the skip lit by two lamps could recover: in *Saper's* case the person who placed the skip was held 60 per cent liable, the car driver 40 per cent liable because of his negligence.

Can the consent of the authority be *assumed*, where contractors are employed to carry out road works? In *A. A. King (Contractors) v. Page* (1970) it was held that in such cases there is an implied authority to carry out all works reasonably necessary to complete the contract so no liability can follow under section 140. But a warning was sounded by the judge in the case: he pointed out that where, as in this case, a metal skip had been left in the road without lights or reflective strips, liability could arise under section 146 of the Highways Act 1949 (failing to light an obstacle at night). So the building contractor may find himself faced with a dual liability where he deposits a skip on the highway.

The contractor in *Gabriel v. Enfield London Borough Council* (1971) attempted to avoid liability, where he hired out skips and deposited them on the highway. He hired them out as rubbish containers, but insisted that customers signed a form to the effect that the driver, when placing the skip in position, was acting as the agent of the customer. This ingenious device failed: it was held that the driver remained the agent of the defendant contractor, so contractor, driver *and* customer were guilty of an offence under section 140.

The Highways Act 1971. Further regulations concerning the placing of skips on highways are found in sections 31 and 32 of the Highways Act 1971. They have the effect of extending and strengthening the section 140 provisions.

Section 31 provides:

(*a*) permission from the authority is needed to deposit a builders' skip on the highway;

(*b*) the permission can include conditions relating to the siting of the skip, its dimensions, the painting of the skip to make it easily visible, the care and disposal of its contents, the manner of its lighting and guarding, and its removal at the end of the period of permission.

The section also states that the owner of the skip which is placed on a highway in accordance with the permission must keep it properly lighted during hours of darkness, must mark it clearly with his name, address and telephone number, must remove it as soon as practicable after it has been filled, and must comply with the conditions laid down – otherwise, he may be found guilty of an offence and fined up to £100. He can escape liability by showing that the offence was due to the act or default of some other person, and that he took all reasonable precautions, and showed all due diligence to avoid the commission of the offence by himself or by persons under his control.

In *York District Council v. Poller* (1975) the district council hired a skip and the skip-owners asked the chief building officer if they could leave the skip in the street. He said there was 'blanket permission' to do so. In fact, an offence was committed under section 31 of the Highways Act 1971. It was held that the *council* was liable for the offence since it was caused by their 'act or default' in saying there was a blanket permit when there was not one.

Section 32 provides:

(a) even where placed on the highway by permission the skip must be removed at the request of the authority or a constable in uniform;

(b) such a request must be complied with as soon as is practicable, and failure to do so may result on conviction in a fine of up to £50;

(c) the authority or the constable in uniform may themselves remove the skip or cause it to be removed or repositioned (and if after due inquiries notification of the owner of the removal, etc., is not possible because he cannot be traced, the skip and its contents can be disposed of);

(d) expenses incurred by the authority or the police can be recovered from the owner.

It should be emphasised that the prudent contractor will avoid risks under the section by consulting the police and the highway authority before placing the skip on the highway, but even so there are those who prefer to run the risk of being caught and prosecuted, with the idea that it might be cheaper that way. But there is more than the fine to be considered; there is the question of legal costs, the firm's reputation and possible civil liability for injury by way of damages. And, as was emphasised in the *Gatland* case: 'Where a person is charged with having deposited, without lawful authority or excuse, anything on the highway,

in consequence whereof a user of the highway is injured or
endangered, commercial convenience is not a valid excuse.'

Section 32 defines a 'builder's skip' as a container designed to be
carried on a road vehicle and to be placed on a highway or other land
for the storage of builders' materials, or for the removal and disposal of
builders' rubble, waste, household and other rubbish or earth. 'Owner'
in relation to a builders' skip hired for not less than one month, means
the person in possession of the skip for that agreement. But it should be
noted that it is not only in the matter of the skips themselves that
contractors may be liable. Under section 140(4) of the Highways Act
1959, 'if a person, without lawful authority or excuse, allows any filth,
dirt, lime or other offensive matter or thing to run or flow on to a
highway from any adjoining premises, he shall be guilty of an offence'.
But such an action may give rise not only to a criminal charge under the
statutory provision; it may give rise to a civil action also.

Common Law Nuisance

An unlawful interference with the highway can result in a civil action –
an action for damages, or for an injunction, or both. Where the
plaintiff sues for damages in such cases he must show, however, that his
injury or loss is substantial and something over and above that suffered
by the public at large. Thus, if the obstruction is temporary, reasonable
in extent and duration, no action will lie, but if these limitations are
exceeded an action is possible and the individual will succeed against
the contractor if he can show particular injury to himself which is the
direct consequence of the wrongful act, and that the injury is of a
substantial character. Thus, in *Chesterfield Corporation v. Arthur Robinson
(Transport) Ltd* (1955) a main road was obstructed for seventy-six hours
because of the defendants' negligent mode of conveying an outsize load
of 83 tons. The plaintiffs succeeded in obtaining damages for the
special loss they had sustained as a result of the diversion of their bus
service. Other examples have arisen as the result of erecting a fence
across a road, narrowing a highway by scaffolding or hoardings and
allowing a structure adjoining a highway to become ruinous and
dangerous. But a highway nuisance cannot be created where the road is
merely under construction: in *Creed v. John McGeoch & Sons Ltd* (1955)
the road had not been dedicated or taken over by the highway authority
so no highway nuisance was created.

As well as, or instead of, asking for damages, the plaintiff may ask for
an injunction, if he has suffered special damage (if he has not, the

Attorney-General must be joined as plaintiff). It may be added that not every interference will require the relation of the Attorney-General. A person who suffers special injury, or has had a particular right infringed, can bring an action in his own right and ask for a declaration, injunction or damages.

Criminal Offences

Proceedings can be taken at common law for a *criminal* as well as a civil offence. In *R. v. Clark* (1964) *C* was indicted on the charge that he had 'unlawfully incited divers persons to commit a nuisance to the public by unlawfully obstructing the highway.' It should be noted, however, that where this kind of case arises a different standard of proof applies from those cases brought under the Highways Act. The presence of *mens rea* is not necessary under section 121 of the 1959 Act, so that where, as in *Arrowsmith v. Jenkins* (1963), it is contended that the defendant did not *intend* to obstruct the highway the contention is irrelevant. The *fact* of obstruction is enough. In the question of a public nuisance by obstruction, on the other hand, though the offence is criminal the question then is whether or not there is a reasonable user of the highway. In *Lowdens v. Keaveney* (1903) it was held there may be a complete obstruction of the highway and yet the *use* to which the street is being put is reasonable. It was this standard which was applied in the public nuisance case of *R. v. Clark* (above), not the standard applying under section 121.

A mitigation of section 121 does arise, however, in the application by the Courts of the *de minimis* rule. If there has been an obstruction section 121 might be applied, but if the obstruction is temporary and insignificant in the circumstances the court might refuse to proceed.

DIVERSION AND EXTINGUISHMENT

The stopping-up or diversion of a highway may be ordered by a magistrates' court if it appears to the court that the highway is unnecessary or diversion would make it nearer, or more commodious, to the public (section 108, Highways Act 1959[12]). The highway authority applies for such orders, but if it is an unclassified road that is concerned the consent of the district council must be obtained, as it must of parish and community councils where they are also involved. An individual may request the authority to start the action, but he may then be called upon to pay the costs involved.

Public path extinguishment orders may be obtained by a county council, district council, the Greater London Council and a National Park joint planning committee if the path in question is not needed for public use. The order must be confirmed by the Secretary of State.

Footpaths and bridle-ways can be diverted where diversion will bring about a more efficient use of the land, or provide a shorter or more commodious route. The county or district council or National Park joint planning board may then make a diversion order. This extinguishes the old right of way and creates a new one. The applicant may be called upon to pay the cost or part of it. A diversion order is ineffective until confirmed by the Secretary of State.

Public rights of way over land purchased under Part III of the Housing Act 1957 (see page 157) can be extinguished by a local authority with the approval of the Secretary of State (objections are dealt with through public inquiry) and section 209 of the Town and Country Planning Act 1971 enables the Secretary of State to authorise stopping-up or diversion of highways to enable development to be carried out in accordance with planning permission granted under Part III of the 1971 Act or carried out by a government department. Planning authorities have similar powers regarding footpaths and bridle-ways (section 210) and highways crossing or entering a proposed new highway route (section 211). Vehicular rights can be extinguished under section 212 to convert a highway into a footpath or bridle-way and local authorities can use this section in respect of areas declared to be general improvement areas under the Housing Act 1969 (see page 52).

STREET LIGHTING

At common law there was no duty to light streets, and in the nineteenth century urban authorities were given power to contract for gas supplies for lighting purposes. The Local Government Acts of 1966 and 1972 now govern the position.

In London the lighting of the metropolitan roads is the responsibility of the Greater London Council; other roads fall to the London boroughs. Outside London the main responsibility lies with the highway authorities (the county councils, and for trunk roads the Secretary of State). Footway lighting, defined by reference to the height and spacing of lamp standards,[13] falls to the lighting authorities –

parish and community councils and parish meetings – who may exercise other lighting powers with the consent of the highway authority.

The fact that the authorities named above have the *power* to light the streets does not make them liable for accidents arising as a result of their failure to do so, but if an authority places an obstruction on the highway it is under a duty to give adequate warning of it. To light it would perhaps be the most effective method, but lighting is not strictly necessary – the duty is merely to take reasonable steps to prevent the obstruction becoming a danger to the public.

STREET CLEANSING

The power to cleanse and water the streets is given to district councils, London borough councils and the Common Council under section 77 of the Public Health Act 1936; they may also be ordered to do this by the Secretary of State. The local authority may arrange for the highway authority to undertake the work, but if it does not the highway authority must make a reasonable contribution to the cost of the work involved. Further powers relating to refuse bins, refuse dumps and litter are given to the authorities by the Public Health Act 1961 and the Control of Pollution Act 1974, the Civic Amenities Act 1967 and the Litter Act 1958.

TRAFFIC MANAGEMENT

General powers are available to local authorities to construct light railways (Light Railways Act 1896), operate tramways and public service vehicles (Road Traffic Act 1930) and to grant travel concessions to 'qualified persons'.

Part II of the Transport Act 1968 enables the Secretary of State for the Environment to designate passenger transport areas in order to effect an integrated and efficient system of public transport. A passenger transport authority and executive may be set up for each area. By section 202 of the Local Government Act 1972 each metropolitan county became a passenger transport area with the metropolitan county council becoming the passenger transport authority. The provision of a co-ordinated and efficient system of passenger transport is made the duty of the metropolitan counties by section 203 of the 1972 Act.

Traffic management functions such as road safety, traffic regulation, waiting restrictions, etc., is the province of the county councils, but with some of the functions, such as the provision of car-parking facilities, there is a sharing of responsibility with the councils of districts, parishes and communities.

Expenditure on maintaining trunk roads can be reimbursed from the Secretary of State and grants are available for cleansing of these roads. Expenditure on principal roads is supported by Exchequer grants (75 per cent on new construction, maintenance, improvement and road lighting installation). Grants may be made under the Highways Act 1959 in respect of approved schemes for new construction and maintenance of special roads and from 1 April 1975 grants have been payable to county councils and the Greater London Council for expenditure for transport purposes. This is defined as expenditure on public transport, highways, traffic regulation and provision of parking places (section 6 of the Local Government Act 1974).

REFERENCES

1. *Cubitt v. Lady Caroline Maxse* (1873), L.R. 8, C.P. 704, p. 705.
2. As amended by the National Parks and Access to the Countryside Act 1949.
3. As amended by the Local Government Act 1972, Schedule 21, para. 13.
4. A road which is an essential route for traffic and which has a sufficiently important place in the national highway system to justify central government interest in its planning and Exchequer assistance towards its improvement: section 27, Local Government Act 1966.
5. Highways (Miscellaneous Provisions) Act 1961, sections 13 and 14; Highways Act 1971, section 51; Land Compensation Act 1973, Schedule 3.
6. As amended by the Local Government Act 1972, Schedule 21, para. 73.
7. By sections 38 and 53 as amended by the Local Government Act 1972, Schedule 21, para. 20; and by section 61 of the Act.
8. *Sharpness New Docks and Gloucester and Birmingham Navigation Co. v. Attorney-General*, [1915] A.C. 654, p. 665, per Lord Atkinson.
9. [1968] 2 All E.R. 343, p. 344.
10. See also *Hubbard and Others v. Pitt and Others* (*The Times*, 12 Nov. 1974) (picketing on highways outside estate agents illegal as not amounting to reasonable passage and repassage).
11. Re-enacting a provision of the Public Utilities Street Works Act 1950; as amended by the Local Government Act 1972, Schedule 21, para. 42.
12. As amended by the Local Government Act 1972, Schedule 21, para. 42.
13. By section 32 of the Local Government Act 1966.

6

Planning Control

The law relating to planning is discovered mainly in the Town and Country Planning Acts of 1971 and 1972 and the Town and Country Amenities Act 1974. The object of the 1974 Act was to make further provision for the control of development in the interests of amenity, and in particular to ensure the protection of trees and the preservation and enhancement of conservation areas, but it also contained important provisions relating to the preservation of buildings of architectural and historic interest, their surroundings and landscapes.

The main provisions relating to planning are found in the 1971 Act, however. The first attempts at systematic planning began in 1909; this was followed by an ever-increasingly complex succession of provisions, but the 1971 legislation consolidated, with amendments, most of the previous statute law.

The practical effect of the law is now to place the good of the community over the rights of the owner to use his land as he pleases. The general principle is that a landowner has no right to use his land for any purpose other than its present use unless he first obtains permission for a change of use. To this must be added the legal right of the authority to take land away from the landowner by compulsory purchase for certain reasons. And planning, as a system, has one further impact to make – that is, upon the economic situation within the community. The existence, or non-existence of planning permission for a piece of land can have great effects upon its market value.

Though planning law is statutory in origin it comes before the courts of law from time to time. But instances are not numerous. The first planning decision is a purely administrative action; a decision reached by a local authority or a government department. An appeal to the Minister will be allowed in many cases and in such circumstance the function of the Minister is quasi-judicial. The decision then reached by the Minister is not, however, one as to legal rights; it is properly one as to the administration of planning policy. To that extent the Minister can be said to be acting as a judge in his own cause. A case in point arose in *Franklin v. Minister of Town and Country Planning* (1948). The Minister publicly stated that Stevenage was to be the first new town under the New Towns Act 1946. He made a draft order to that effect and an inquiry was held to take account of the objections to the order. The Minister later confirmed the order. The court held that there was no *judicial* duty placed upon the Minister: his duty was to *consider* the objections only. His decision would be taken after such consideration, but effectively he was implementing policy, not acting as a judge.

The very fact that there was a court action thereafter illustrates that a limited right of appeal against Ministerial decisions exists. The power of the High Court to review decisions and orders will be dealt with later.

THE PLANNING AUTHORITIES

The local planning authorities are county councils and district councils. The planning functions are divided between them as follows:

(a) county planning authorities are responsible for the preparation of structure plans (see page 111) and development plan schemes in consultation with district planning authorities;

(b) district planning authorities, subject to any provision to the contrary in the structure plan or development plan scheme, are responsible for the preparation of local plans.

Effectively, this means that the district planning authorities deal directly with most matters of planning control within their areas, while the county planning authorities are concerned with the general strategy of planning policy.

Greater London

The Greater London Council is the planning authority for Greater London as a whole but the London boroughs and the Common Council of the City of London are planning authorities for all purposes except:

(a) that development specified by regulation by the Minister; and

(b) development plans where there is a division of responsibility with the Greater London Council.

Joint Boards

A joint board may be established by order of the Secretary of State as the planning authority for the area of two or more counties or parts of counties. He may also, in the same way, establish a joint board as the planning authority for districts. If the councils concerned have not agreed to the order the Secretary of State must first hold a local inquiry. In national parks all planning functions fall to the county planning authority or the joint board as the case may be, though there are a few exceptions to this.

The Minister Responsible

While the Secretary of State for Trade and Industry has some responsibilities in respect of the distribution of industry and office development the Secretary of State for the Environment is given the duty, by section 1 of the Minister of Town and Country Planning Act 1943, of 'securing consistency and continuity in the framing and execution of a national policy with respect to the use and development of land throughout England and Wales' and is therefore the Minister mainly concerned with planning. The Town and Country Planning Acts contain many statutory powers of a specific nature which are exercisable by him and these include default powers so that if, for instance, a local planning authority fails to submit a local plan after a specified period he may prepare one himself, as he may alter a structure plan if the authority fails to make necessary alterations.

THE SYSTEM OF CONTROL

A primary creative duty of the planning authority is to produce at periodic intervals plans for future development in its area. Under the Town and Country Planning Act 1962 a development plan was to be prepared to indicate how the authority proposed that land within its area should be used, and the stages by which that development should be carried out.

The Town and Country Planning Act 1968 introduced a new system of development plans; the provisions, which are now contained in Part II of the 1971 Act, will progressively replace the 1962 provisions as the Secretary of State brings them into operation in various areas.

Development Plans under the 1962 Act

The Town and Country Planning Act 1962 imposed on local planning authorities a duty to survey their areas and report to the Secretary of State, submitting a development plan for the areas which was to indicate the uses proposed for land in the areas and the stages by which development was to be carried out. The approved plan would then act as the basis for development control by the planning authority. It did not in itself *authorise* development. Preparation or amendment of a county plan could take place only after consultation between the planning authority and any county district included in the plan.

The Act called for the review of the plans every five years, though amendments could be submitted to the Secretary of State at any time. It was also open to him to direct the planning authority to submit alterations or additions to the plan.

The development plans consist of written statements and maps. Each plan will define the sites of proposed roads, public buildings, open spaces, etc., and will allocate areas of land for agricultural, residential, industrial and other specified purposes, as well as areas of comprehensive development.

Areas of comprehensive development are those areas which require to be developed or re-developed as a whole for any purpose specified in the plan. In particular, regard is had to those areas where extensive war damage was caused, or where conditions of bad layout, or obsolete development occurred, or where the relocation of population, or industry, or the replacement of open space in the course of development or redevelopment of any other area, arose.

The Development Plans Regulations 1965 provided, *inter alia*, for notices to be placed in the press of the submission of a plan, or of proposals to amend a plan. Under the regulations the plans must be made available for public inspection. In preparing and amending the plans objections and representations must be taken into consideration and local inquiries are to be held to deal with objections to the proposals. Once the plans are approved, copies, including maps, are to be available for sale at reasonable cost.

Development Plans under the 1971 Act

The new system is being applied gradually to individual areas designated by statutory commencement orders. It involves the preparation of structure and local plans. The Town and Country Planning (Structure and Local Plans) Regulations 1972 lay down the form and contents of structure and local plans and detail the procedure to be followed in their preparation, submission, withdrawal, approval, adoption, alteration, repeal and replacement.

Survey The first step to be undertaken by the planning authority is a survey of its area, to examine matters likely to affect the development of the area, and to keep these matters under review. A survey may have already been made; this can be used, unless the Secretary of State directs a new survey to be made. The matters the authority will take into consideration in the survey will include physical and economic characteristics, population factors, communications, transport facilities and traffic.

Consultation Before reaching a decision as to the content of the structure or local plan the planning authority must consult the council of any county district to which the plan relates, and such other authorities or bodies as the planning authority considers appropriate, or as the Secretary of State may direct. Where the plans will embrace land lying in a designated national park, or within an area of outstanding natural beauty, or where the plans cover coasts of particular scenic quality (the 'heritage coasts') the planning authority will also consult the Countryside Commission.

Structure Plans After the survey is completed, representations considered, planning policies taken into account and relevant bodies consulted, the planning authority will undertake the preparation of the structure plan. In this structure plan the authority must set out its 'policy and general proposals' for the development and other use of the land in the area. It will include measures for the improvement of the physical environment and the management of traffic. It will state how these proposals relate to proposals for neighbouring areas and will have regard to regional policies and the resources likely to be available for the implementation of the proposals. It will indicate 'action areas' but it will not show the effect of proposals upon particular pieces of land.

The structure plan itself will consist of a written statement which will set out the policy and the proposals, and contain an explanation and a reasoned justification for them. The statement itself will be accompanied by a 'key diagram' which will show the main proposals in the form of a diagram, though the detail or plotting to scale expected of an Ordnance Survey map is not required.

The Secretary of State may approve the plan in whole or in part, with or without modifications, and with or without reservations. In considering the plan he will take into account any objections raised.

Under the Town and Country Planning (Amendment) Act 1972 joint structure plans may be prepared for combined areas. The Act also allows the withdrawal of structure plans and provides for a mandatory examination in public of matters selected by the Secretary of State contained in any structure plan submitted for approval.

'Action areas' are those areas where comprehensive change by way of development, redevelopment or improvement is expected to begin within ten years from the date on which the structure plan is submitted to the Secretary of State for approval.

The essential role of the structure plan is, then, to set out against a background of economic and social considerations the physical, transportation and environmental policies and proposals for the area, and the most effective ways of dealing with them. On the basis of the structure plan decisions can then be taken which can give effect to approved regional strategies, and which can provide a broad basis for detailed local planning. The structure plan is also the means by which the statutory development-control machinery can be exercised – by way of applications for planning permission, and appeals, for instance – and it also provides a general guide to persons interested in development or conservation.

Local Plans. The structure plan deals with issues at the level of policy or general proposals. By section 11 of the 1971 Act the local planning authority may prepare a local plan at any time after the preparation of the structure plan. When the structure plan has been approved the planning authority *may* prepare the local plan to conform generally with the structure plan, for any part of its area; where the Secretary of State so directs it *must* prepare such a local plan.

Section 11 and regulation 15 provide for three kinds of local plans. They may be *district* plans, which are designed for areas where the factors in local planning need to be set out comprehensively; *action area* plans, which again provide for comprehensive planning, but which are designed for those areas which are selected for intensive change by development, redevelopment or improvement, or a combination of these methods; or *subject* plans, which are designed to enable particular aspects or issues to be given detailed treatment.

The local plan comprises a map and written statement and map, and such diagrams, illustrations and descriptive matter as the authority considers appropriate. It formulates the planning authority's proposals for the development and other use of land in that part of the area and indicates the measures that the authority considers fit to include for the improvement of the physical environment and the management of traffic. They are thus designed to take matters one step further from the structure plan by elaborating the general proposals in detail for particular areas. Like the old development plans local plans bring out the effect of planning proposals upon individual properties and include an Ordnance Survey-based map.

Different local plans may be prepared for different purposes for the same part of a local planning authority's area.

Local plans go through the same process of preparation as the structure plans, including consultation, publicity and public participation.

Publicity and Public Participation. Adequate publicity must be given to the report of the survey. The matters proposed to be contained in a structure plan and in a local plan must be publicised before drafting of the final plan and the public must be informed of its rights to make representations. The authority must take such representations into consideration and the Secretary of State must be satisfied that this has been done. The period within which representation may be made must be not less than six weeks from publication of the proposals.

When structure plans have been submitted to the Secretary of State they must be made available for public inspection, as must copies of local plans as finally prepared. They must be accompanied by a statement of the time, which must be at least six weeks, during which objections may be made.

Default. By section 17 of the 1971 Act, where an authority fails to carry out a survey or prepare or submit any structure or local plan, or proposals for alteration, when required to do so, the Secretary of State, after holding a local inquiry, can undertake the work in default. Alternatively, he may authorise another local planning authority which appears to have an interest in the proper planning of the area to undertake the work.

Objections to Structure Plans. Objections to a structure plan must be made to the Secretary of State. He must, by section 9(3) of the 1971 Act,[1] consider these objections and hold an examination in public of matters affecting his consideration of the plan. The main purpose of the examination is to provide him with the information and arguments he needs to reach a decision, and he will select matters on the structure plan itself, the local authority's statement about publicity and public participation and consultation, and on the objections and representations made. At least six weeks' notice of the examination in public must be given, by advertisement, and the proceedings are conducted by a panel chaired by a person appointed by the Secretary of State.[2] The panel reports to the Secretary of State, who will publish any new information coming to him, advertise any formal modifications he proposes to make (for purposes of further objections and representations) and will finally give a reasoned decision, which will form part of the plan.

A person aggrieved by the structure plan as approved by the Secretary of State can raise the matter in the High Court on two grounds only:

(*a*) the plan itself, or some provision in the plan, is *ultra vires*;

(*b*) one of the procedural requirements has not been complied with.

Any such application to the High Court must be made within six weeks of the approval by the Secretary of State and if the applicant proves his point to the satisfaction of the court the plan, or the relevant part of it, may be quashed. By section 242 of the 1971 Act the plan cannot be questioned in any other legal proceedings and it will come into operation on the date that notice is given of approval by the Secretary of State.

Modifications and Alterations. If the Secretary of State proposes to modify a structure plan he must notify the local planning authority, unless he is satisfied that his proposals will not materially affect the plan's content. The local authority must advertise the proposals and serve notice of the proposals on any person(s) nominated by the Secretary of State. If a local authority wishes to modify its local plan the modifications must be published and objections to them considered. The authority may hold a public local inquiry into such objections, and must do so if required by the Secretary of State.

Proposals for alterations to an approved structure plan can be submitted by the local planning authority at any time as the authority thinks fit, or as the Secretary of State directs. This is a departure from the 1962 system, where quinquennial reviews were obligatory. Proposals for alteration to local plan may also be made at any time. The procedures to be followed in these cases are roughly the same as those to be followed in preparation of plans.

Objections to Local Plans. Objections to local plans must be made to the planning authority, not to the Secretary of State. Objectors have a right to be heard at a public local inquiry or other hearing. The local planning authority must consider the inspector's report on a local plan and decide whether or not to take action upon his recommendations.

Obligations to Purchase. In some circumstances public authorities may be called upon by private owners to purchase interests affected by proposals appearing in the structure plan or local plan. Thus, for instance, an owner-occupier who wishes to sell his property but is unable to do so except at a price much lower than he could otherwise expect because it is liable to be purchased compulsorily by a public authority can call upon the authority to purchase his property at once. This, and other circumstances relating to compulsory purchase, will be dealt with more conveniently in the next chapter.

DEVELOPMENT CONTROL

Development of land cannot be undertaken unless planning permission has been given to do so. Part III of the 1971 Act and the regulations made under it make provision for control of development by means of local planning authorities, with a number of powers being conferred on the Secretary of State, to whom appeals against planning decisions may be made.

Definition of Development

Section 22 of the 1971 Act defines 'development' as 'the carrying out of building, engineering, mining or other operations in, on, over or under land, or the making of any material change in the use of buildings or other land'.

The meaning of 'building' in this sense was considered in *Cheshire County Council v. Woodward* (1962) a case involving the Ministerial decision that a hopper and conveyor, which were on wheels but could not be moved about the yard, were not 'buildings'. 'Building', it was held, does not amount to 'development' unless it changes the physical character of the land and there is only one test of this: where the new structure is affixed to the land it will in general be part of the land and will constitute development, but if it is intended to move about and can be wheeled on or off the land its installation will not amount to development – though all circumstances must be taken into consideration.

The question whether a change of use is a 'material change' is largely a matter of fact and degree. The courts have taken the view that they will allow appeals on such matters only where the decision is one which the Minister could not have reached if he had properly directed himself as to the law. Thus, in *Bendles Motors v. Bristol Corporation* (1963) the Divisional Court stated that though they would have reached a different decision than the Minister (who had decided that the placing of an egg-vending machine in the forecourt of a service station amounted to a material change of use) they would not interfere with that decision.

Certain operations and uses are deemed not to involve development for the purposes of the Act. These are:

(1) works of maintenance, improvement or other alteration which affect the *interior* of a building or do not affect materially the external appearance, unless the alteration provides additional space below ground;

(2) road repairs and improvements by a highway authority within the boundaries of a road;

(3) repairs to public services such as sewers and water mains;

(4) the use of buildings or other land within the curtilage of a dwelling-house for a purpose incidental to the enjoyment of the use;

(5) the use of land for agriculture or forestry;

(6) a change of use within a specified 'use class'.

The Use Classes

The use classes mentioned in (6) above are contained in the Town and Country Planning (Use Classes) Order 1972, which lists a number of classes where a change from one use to another, if within one of the classes, is deemed not to be development. For example, a building used for light industry may be used for another type of light industry without the need to apply for planning permission. Particular reference is made to shops and their change of use.

Material Change of Use

It is not always easy to decide what constitutes a material change of use, as has already been mentioned. By section 22(3) of the 1971 Act the use as more than one separate dwelling of a building previously used as a single dwelling does not amount to a material change of use, while again, tipping on what is already a tip is development if the height is raised or the area of the tip extended. But the test as to whether there has been a material change of use depends upon the character of the use – not the particular purpose of the individual occupier. An intensification of use may well amount to a material change of use. In *Birmingham Corporation v. Minister of Housing and Local Government and Habib Ullah* (1963) the Minister decided that where a single family let out some of the house as lodgings this would not be a material change of use, but on appeal it was held that there could be development in such circumstances if the change was sufficiently marked. In this case an appeal had been lodged against the planning authority's decision to the Minister (now the Secretary of State) and a further appeal was made to the High Court, against the Minister's decision. This procedure constitutes the appellate system against the local planning authority's decision.

Permitted Development

Section 24 of the 1971 Act empowers the Secretary of State to make development orders. These have the effect of granting development consent and examples are provided by the Town and Country Planning (New Towns Special Development) Order 1963 and the Town and Country Planning General Development Order 1973. The 1973 order specifies classes of development which are permitted by the order itself and which may be carried out by a developer without obtaining consent from the local planning authority or from the Secretary of State, though he may need consent under some other statutory provision. The main classes are as follows:

Class I

(1) The enlargement, improvement or other alteration of a dwelling-house provided there is no increase in cubic capacity exceeding $49 \cdot 5$ cubic metres or 10 per cent, whichever is the greater, up to a maximum increase of 113 cubic metres. Enlargement may include the erection of garages, stables, loose-boxes or coach-houses within the grounds of the dwelling-house provided they do not exceed the height of the house itself or project beyond its front, and porches, hardstandings and oil tanks which satisfy the specified conditions.

(2) The erection, construction, placing, maintenance or improvement or other alteration, of any building, or enclosure (other than a dwelling, garage, stable, loose-box or coach-house) within the grounds of a dwelling-house for any purpose incidental to the

enjoyment of the dwelling-house as such, including the keeping
of pets, livestock and the like, for the domestic needs or personal
enjoyment of the occupants of the dwelling-house, provided that
the height of any such building does not exceed 3 metres (3·6
metres if it has a ridged roof).

Class II

(1) The erection or construction of gates, fences, walls, or other
means of enclosure not exceeding 7 feet in height (4 feet where
they abut on a road used by vehicular traffic); and the maintenance, or the improvement or other alteration of such means of
enclosure, provided the height is not thereby increased above
the height appropriate for a new means of enclosure.
(2) The painting of the exterior of a building otherwise than for
purposes of advertisement, announcement or direction.

Class III

Change of use from general industry to light industry; or from use as a
fried-fish shop, tripe shop, cats' meat shop, shop for the sale of pets or
shop for the sale of motor vehicles to use as any other kind of shop.

Class IV

(1) The erection of temporary structures required in connection with
building, engineering or other operations (other than mining
operations) for which planning permission has been or is deemed
to be granted, provided that the structures are removed when the
operations are completed and that, where they have been erected
on land adjoining the actual operations the land is reinstated
immediately.
(2) Temporary use of land for all purposes (except as a caravan site)
is limited, cumulatively, to a total of 28 days in any calendar year[3],
and the erection or placing of moveable structures on the land
for the purposes of that use. This is intended for travelling fairs,
shows, camping and similar purposes.

Class VIII

The carrying out on land used for industrial purposes of certain
specified works in connection with that use, including the extension or
alteration of buildings (subject to limitations as to height and cubic

content), and including the continued use as a waste tip of any land comprised in a site which was in use for that purpose on 1 July 1948.

Class IX

The carrying out of works required for the maintenance or improvement of a private road, provided such works are carried out on land within the boundaries of the road.

Class X

The carrying out of works required for the inspection, repair, or renewal of sewers, mains and similar services.

Class XI

The rebuilding, restoration, or replacement of war-damaged buildings, works or plant, provided that there is no increase in their cubic content except such as is permitted under Class I or Class VIII and that any material alteration in external appearance shall be subject to the approval of the local planning authority.

Certain standard conditions apply to the classes of development noted above. These are two in number:

1. Development must not involve the formation, laying out or material widening of a means of access to a trunk or classified road.
2. Development must not cause dangerous obstruction to the view of persons using a road used by vehicular traffic at or near any bend, corner, junction or intersection.

Planning Permission

Except in those cases covered by 'permitted development' under the General Development Orders it is necessary for planning permission for any development to be obtained from the local planning authority, which may grant it, conditionally or unconditionally, or may refuse it.

The local planning authority, in dealing with such applications, must have regard to the development or structure plan and to any other material consideration. By section 35 of the 1971 Act the Secretary of State may give directions that any application or class of applications shall be referred to him for decision.

In general the district planning authorities deal with:

(a) applications for planning permission;

(*b*) applications for determination as to whether permission is required; and

(*c*) applications for a certificate of established use.

It deals with all cases which do not relate to 'county matters' – that is, matters such as mineral working; development which would seriously conflict with or prejudice the implementation of fundamental provisions of the structure plan; development which would be inconsistent with the provisions of a local plan; development which would be inconsistent with declared planning policies of the county planning authority; development which has been prescribed, or which is in a class prescribed, by the Secretary of State by order.

Procedure. The applications are normally addressed to the local planning authority to which the planning authority has delegated the function of receiving such applications. It is not necessary that the applicant possesses a legal interest in the land in question so applications may be made by prospective purchasers.

Applications must normally be made on the prescribed form and be accompanied by detailed plans and drawings of the proposed development. An alternative form of application is possible, however; namely, an application for outline permission which is submitted in respect of the erection of buildings. Outline planning applications need be accompanied only by a site plan.

Where outline permission is granted, details of the proposed development must be approved by the authority within a prescribed period before the actual work is begun. This is known as approval of reserved matters. (The period is five years for ordinary planning permission; three years for approval of matters reserved.) The alternative procedure is available so that a prospective purchaser of property may obtain a preliminary decision regarding development without having to prepare detailed building plans. Where the authority's decision is likely to depend upon the design or appearance of the development, however, the authority may refuse to give outline permission and may insist upon submission of a planning application proper.

Decisions must be reached within two months; applicants may lodge an appeal with the Secretary of State if his application has been refused. If the applicant is not the owner of the property in question he must inform the owner of the application. Where the land is agricultural land both owner and tenant must be notified.

Every planning permission is subject to the condition that the development will be begun within five years of the date of the grant of permission, unless the permission itself stipulates a shorter or longer period. In the case of outline planning permission application for approval of any matters reserved for subsequent approval must be made within three years of the date of the grant of outline permission, and the development must be begun within five years of the grant of outline permission, or within two years from the final approval of reserved matters, whichever is the later. Where development has begun within the time limit but it appears that it will not be completed within a reasonable period the local planning authority may issue a 'completion notice'. This notice, which must be confirmed by the Secretary of State, will specify a further time limit of not less than twelve months after which the planning permission will cease to have effect in so far as it authorises development not carried out within the time limit.

Applications in respect of certain kinds of development must be advertised by the applicant in a local newspaper and a notice must also be placed on the land in question. These classes of development are designated in the Town and Country Planning General Development Order 1973 and include the erection of such buildings as public conveniences, slaughterhouses, knackers' yards, theatres, cinemas, dance halls, music halls, skating-rinks, swimming-baths, turkish baths, gymnasia, buildings for indoor games or for use as scrap yards or coal yards or disposal of refuse, and the construction of buildings higher than twenty metres.

In all these cases the application must be accompanied by a certificate which must state: either

(a) that the applicant is the owner or tenant of the whole of the land; or

(b) that he has notified those owners whose names and addresses he knows, and has advertised the application; or

(c) that he has notified all the owners.

He must, additionally, certify either that the land does not form part of an agricultural holding, or that he has notified any agricultural tenant. Representations which are received within twenty-one days of the publication of the advertisement or the notification must be considered by the local planning authority before a decision is arrived at.

The local planning authority must maintain a register of applications for planning permission made to that authority, with information as to how the applications have been dealt with. The register, which must include copies of current applications and plans and drawings submitted with them, must be available for inspection by the public at all reasonable hours.

Conditional Permission

It has already been stated that planning permission may be granted subject to conditions including conditions which limit the period for which it is granted, and requiring the developer to remove any buildings or works authorised, and reinstate the land at the end of the period. The legitimate scope of such conditions and the effect on the validity of the permission where a condition has been declared *ultra vires* have been considered by the courts. Cases dealt with in the late 1950s[4] established the following principles:

(1) A condition must 'fairly and reasonably relate' to the permitted development – it must serve some useful planning purpose.
(2) If a condition does fairly and reasonably relate to the permitted development the court will not enquire further into its reasonableness.
(3) A condition may be imposed restricting the user of premises according to the personal circumstances of the occupier.
(4) A condition will be declared invalid on the ground that its meaning is uncertain.

In the first of these cases, Lord Denning said:[5]

Although the planning authorities are given very wide powers to impose 'such conditions as they think fit', nevertheless the law says that those conditions, to be valid, must fairly and reasonably relate to the permitted development. The planning authority are not at liberty to use their powers for an ulterior object, however desirable that object may seem to them to be in the public interest.

But what is the situation where the condition imposed is *ultra vires*? What effect does this have on the planning permission itself? In *Hall & Co. v. Shoreham-by-Sea Urban District Council* (1964) the condition attached to the planning permission was that the applicant company constructed a service road and give right of passage over it to and from such ancillary roads as might be constructed on adjoining land. The council refused to enforce closure of a new 'temporary' access to the land until the service and ancillary roads were constructed. The Court of Appeal held that these conditions were *ultra vires* and void for unreasonableness because they required the company to construct a road on their own land and dedicate it to the public without compensation. But as these conditions were fundamental to the grant of planning permission they could not merely be severed, leaving the planning permission valid; they were void, and the permission itself was also void.

It follows from this that much depends upon the court's view as to whether the condition attached is *fundamental* to the planning permission or not. If it is, the permission itself must also be invalidated where the condition is *ultra vires*. If in the court's view the condition is *not* fundamental, and it can be severed without detriment, its invalidity as being *ultra vires* will not affect the planning permission itself, which will still stand. Circular 5/68 issued by the Ministry of Housing and Local Government and entitled 'The Use of Conditions in Planning Permissions' contains guidance on the use of powers to impose conditions on planning permissions and sets out general principles.

Controls in Special Cases

Special provisions apply to certain applications for planning permission.

1. *Industrial Building.* Where an application for consent relates to the erection of an industrial building the change of use of existing premises to such a building, or the retention of a building for industrial purposes which will by itself, or together with other development relating to the same building or another in the same group, cover a floor space of more than 464 square metres (or other area fixed by regulation)[6] the application must be accompanied by an industrial development certificate. This is obtained from the Department of Trade and Industry and certifies that the erection of the building can be carried out consistently with the proper distribution of industry.

In deciding whether or not a certificate should be granted the Department of Trade and Industry must have regard to the need for providing appropriate employment in development areas – that is, areas of high unemployment. Restrictions may be attached to the certificate: these must be observed by the applicant when he makes a planning application. The department may also attach conditions which the planning authority will be bound to include in any planning permission granted.

2. *Office Development.* Office development in the metropolitan area in the south-east of England is controlled, and this control, under sections 73 to 85 of the 1971 Act, may be extended to other areas by order of the Department of Trade and Industry. The control, which is due to end on 5 August 1977 or such earlier date as may be specified by Order in Council, means that planning consent may not be granted for development which involves the erection or extension of, or the change of use of existing premises to, office premises unless the application is accompanied by an office development permit supplied by the Department of Trade and Industry. The department, in issuing such permits, has regard to the need for promoting the better distribution of employment in Great Britain. Restrictions and conditions may be attached to the office development permits.

Office development which does not exceed specified limits of floor space is exempt. The area specified by the Control of Office Development (Exemption Limit) Order 1970 is 10,000 square feet.

3. *Development by Local Authorities and Statutory Undertakers.* If the proposed development requires the authorisation of a government department the department can give the planning consent along with the authorisation. Where a local planning authority proposes to develop within its area the permission of the Secretary of State is required. If the development is contrary to provisions contained in the development plan an application is made to the authority and under section 35 of the 1971 Act this application is deemed to be referred to the Secretary of State. Where, on the other hand, the development is in accordance with the development plan it is not necessary to notify the Secretary of State; permission is deemed to have been granted. Most of the ordinary development carried out by local authorities and by statutory undertakers is permitted development.

4. *Other Special Controls.* A number of other special controls by way of specific powers and duties are imposed upon local planning authorities. They include:

(*a*) powers and duties relating to the preservation and replacement of trees and woodlands (see page 142):

(*b*) powers and duties relating to the preservation of buildings and areas of special architectural or historic interest (see page 137);

(*c*) power to control outdoor advertisements (see page 144);

(*d*) power to require gardens, vacant sites, or other open land in their area to be put in good order within a specified period so as not to injure the amenity of the area; and

(*e*) powers and duties relating to the dumping of refuse.

5. *Listed Buildings.* An important control exists in relation to buildings of special architectural or historic interest as far as demolition, alteration or extension is concerned. Such works require a 'listed building consent' from the local planning authority, or in some cases from the Secretary of State. The consent may have conditions attached to it relating to particular features of the building, the making good of any damage caused by the works or the reconstruction of the building with the use of original materials so far as is practicable. If demolition and redevelopment is intended listed building consent to demolition must be obtained in addition to planning permission for the new building, but where the listed building is to be extended or altered specific planning permission for the proposed works can also operate as listed building consent. The matter is dealt with in more detail on page 137.

APPEALS

Where permission to develop has been refused by a local planning authority, or where permission has been granted but subject to conditions, a right of appeal exists to the Secretary of State and in certain cases to the High Court.

Appeals to the Secretary of State

Where an appeal is made to the Secretary of State he may refuse to entertain it where the case is one that appears to him to be an instance where the local planning authority has no power to grant the permission, or to grant it without imposing the conditions appealed against.

An appeal can be made to the Secretary of State, additionally to the circumstances mentioned above, if within such period prescribed by a development order the local planning authority has neither given a decision on an application by granting planning permission nor referred it to the Secretary of State. The General Development Orders lay down the period as two months, or three months in the case of development affecting a trunk road, or such longer periods as may be agreed between the applicant and the local planning authority.

Notice of appeal must be given to the Secretary of State within six months, or such longer period as he may allow, from receipt of the notice of the decision, or from expiry of the period within which the decision should have been given.

Before reaching a decision on the appeal the Secretary of State must allow both the applicant and the local authority the opportunity of being heard by a person appointed by him, if they so desire. In many cases a public local inquiry is held by a Departmental Inspector. The Secretary of State may allow the appeal, or dismiss it, or may vary any part of the local planning authority's decision.

By section 50 of the Town and Country Planning Act 1971 an independent tribunal may be established to hear appeals against decisions of local planning authorities relating to the design and external appearance of buildings. Sections 47 to 49 of the Act provide for the constitution of Planning Inquiry Commissions to conduct special planning inquiries in place of normal departmental inquiries, in prescribed circumstances where the proposed development involves matters of national or regional importance, or technical or scientific issues of an unfamiliar character.

Appeals to the High Court

An appeal may be made to the High Court against certain orders made by a local planning authority or the Secretary of State under the development control provisions, and against certain actions taken by the Secretary of State under those provisions.

By section 245 of the 1971 Act the appeal can be made in respect of specified orders, decisions or directions made by the local planning authority or the Secretary of State; they include:

(a) orders revoking or modifying planning permission;
(b) orders for discontinuance of a use of land;
(c) tree-preservation orders;
(d) orders relating to buildings of architectural or historic interest;
(e) orders relating to special control of advertisements.

The actions of the Secretary of State which may be appealed against are:

(a) decisions on appeals against refusal or conditional grant of planning permission;
(b) decisions against enforcement notices or listed building enforcement notices;

(*c*) decisions on applications for planning permission referred to him;

(*d*) confirmation of purchase notices (see below, p. 128);

(*e*) decisions in connection with tree-preservation orders or advertisements;

(*f*) directions as to the review of planning decisions where compensation is claimed;

(*g*) decisions on appeals against certificates of appropriate alternative development in compulsory purchase cases (see page 174).[7]

The person who is aggrieved by such orders or actions and who wishes to question the validity of the matter on the ground that it is *ultra vires*, or that the statutory requirements have not been complied with, must make his appeal to the High Court within six weeks of the date of confirmation of the order or action taken. This time limit applies also to any local authority, statutory undertaker or local planning authority that wishes to appeal.

An appeal to the High Court on a point of law lies from a decision of the Secretary of State on an appeal against an enforcement notice (see below) or a listed building enforcement notice; such an appeal also lies against a determination of the Secretary of State under section 53 of the 1971 Act as to whether a given set of facts constitutes development (where he has dealt with the matter on appeal from a local planning authority decision under section 36, or where it comes to him under a section 35 appeal). Alternatively an aggrieved person may require the Secretary of State to state a case for the opinion of the High Court.

Purchase Notices

A further remedy is available to an aggrieved person under sections 180 to 187 of the 1971 Act. The local planning authority may have granted permission subject to conditions, or it may have refused permission to develop. If the owner is able to claim, as a result of this action, that the land has become incapable of reasonably beneficial use he may serve a 'purchase notice' on the district council calling upon the authority to purchase his interest in the land.

Where the authority is prepared to accept the notice the authority is deemed to be authorised to acquire the interest compulsorily. Where the authority is not prepared to accept the notice a copy of it is sent to the Secretary of State by the authority; he may then confirm it, or confirm it with a direction that some other authority shall be required to buy the land: the education authority, for example. He may also, as an alternative, grant the permission which the local authority refused, or may vary the conditions, or grant permission for other development.

The test as to whether the existing land has become incapable of reasonably beneficial use or not was considered in *R. v. Minister of Housing and Local Government,* ex p. *Chichester Rural District Council* (1960) where the Minister confirmed the notice on the ground that 'the land in its existing state and with the benefit of temporary planning permission . . . is of substantially less use and value to its owner than it would be if planning permission had been granted'. The court held the Minister's reason to be invalid – the question was not whether the land was of less use to the owner, but whether it had become incapable of beneficial use in its existing state.

The Secretary of State is bound to give notice of his proposed action, and if so requested he must arrange for a hearing or a local inquiry. In determining what constitutes a reasonably beneficial use of the land no account must be taken of any prospective use which would involve the carrying out of 'new development' – that is, development which is not within the 'existing use' categories in Schedule 8 to the 1971 Act.

REVOCATION AND MODIFICATION

Where permission has been given for development and the land in question has been sold the planning consent that has been given may be taken advantage of by the new owner of the land, for unless the contrary is stated a planning consent attaches to the land, for the benefit of that land and all persons for the time being interested in it.

This does not, however, prevent a local planning authority later revoking the consent or modifying it. By sections 45 and 46 of the 1971 Act where the works to which the consent has been given are not completed, or a change of use has not been effected, the local planning authority may revoke or modify the consent already given. The order of revocation or modification will not become effective until the Secretary of State has confirmed it, and it should be noted that compensation is payable. An unopposed order which does not involve the payment of compensation may become operative, after due advertisement, without the confirmation of the Secretary of State.

The person affected by the order and claiming compensation can claim for any abortive expenditure he has incurred, or in respect of any other loss or damage sustained by reason of the revocation or modification. In assessing the amount payable by way of compensation existing rights may be taken into account.

Local planning authorities may also order the discontinuance of any existing use of land, or the modification of existing use by imposing conditions, or by ordering removal or alteration of buildings or works on the land. Such orders must be confirmed by the Secretary of State and compensation is payable for any reduction in the existing use value of the land and for any disturbance resulting from the requirement. In certain cases accommodation must be provided for persons displaced from their residences. Purchase notices can sometimes be served where an authority takes action in this way.

ENFORCEMENT OF PLANNING CONTROL

The enforcement provisions are contained in sections 87 to 95 of the 1971 Act. If any development or use of land takes place without planning permission having first been obtained, or in contravention of conditions which have been attached to the permission which has been obtained, the local planning authority may serve an enforcement notice on the owner and occupier of the land concerned, and on any other person having an interest in the land materially affected.

The notice will specify the breach of planning control which has taken place and will require steps to be taken to (*a*) restore the land to its previous state, or (*b*) discontinue the use, or (*c*) comply with the conditions. The notice may also require the removal of any buildings erected without permission.

Where the breach of control consists in the erection of buildings or the carrying out of engineering, mining or other operations without permission the notice must be served within four years of the date of the breach. The four-year limitation also applies where there has been failure to comply with a planning condition, or where there has been change of use of a building without permission to use as a single dwelling-house. No time limit applies where other unauthorised changes of use occur – the only limitation which applies is that the breach must have commenced after 1963.

Appeals

Two periods are specified in the notice. The first period, of not less than twenty-eight days, is the period at the end of which the notice takes effect. The second period stated is the period allowed for compliance with the notice.

During the first period stated the owner or occupier or other person having an interest in the land may make an appeal against the enforcement notice to the Secretary of State on any of the following grounds:

   (1) that the matters alleged in the notice do not constitute a breach of planning control;

   (2) that in the case of development or a condition involving building, engineering, mining or other operations the four-year period has expired;

   (3) that in any other case the breach of control was out of time because it began before 1964;

   (4) that the notice was not properly served;

   (5) that the requirements of the notice are excessive;

   (6) that the period allowed for compliance is too short.

The appellant may also ask the Secretary of State to grant permission for the development to which the notice relates, or to discharge the condition which has been infringed and this enables the Secretary of State to judge the merit of the development to which the enforcement notice relates. He can then grant permission if he so chooses.

Where an appeal is made, the applicant is deemed to have made application for planning permission for the development to which the enforcement notice relates. The enforcement notice in itself cannot become effective where an appeal has been lodged until such time as the appeal is decided. Once the enforcement notice has become effective the planning authority may, if the notice is not complied with, enter upon the land after giving reasonable notice and take steps to enforce the notice by restoring the land as required under the notice. Costs can be charged to the owner. In *Arcam Demolition and Construction Co. v. Worcestershire County Council* (1964) a landowner moved for an injunction to restrain the planning authority which intended entering onto the land to carry out only *part* of the works required by a previously served enforcement notice. The court held the authority was within the rights granted by the Act and no injunction should be granted.

As an alternative to entry upon the land, or additionally to that remedy, the authority may take proceedings in the magistrates' court against any person who owned the land when the notice was served. The court can impose a fine not exceeding £400, and £50 for every day the contravention continues. But if the enforcement notice required the discontinuance of a use, or if the contravention related to a breach of a condition, proceedings may be taken for a fine only against any person who uses or permits the land to be used in a way which contravenes the notice.

If the enforcement notice is materially defective and a nullity the person on whom it is served can ignore it and if prosecuted can challenge its validity, but under section 88(4) of the 1971 Act the Secretary of State has power to correct on appeal any informality, defect or error, if he is satisfied that it is not material.

In *Kingston upon Thames Royal London Borough Council v. Secretary of State for the Environment* (1974) an enforcement notice was quashed under section 88 but the council appealed to the High Court[8] on the ground that the Secretary of State had erred in law. The council argued that the condition imposed in the enforcement notice had been *ultra vires*. The Secretary of State relied upon section 29(1)(*a*) of the 1971 Act,[9] which gives local authorities almost limitless powers to impose conditions, albeit judicially restricted by principles laid down in the *Pyx Granite* and *Fawcett Properties* cases (see pages 131, 153). The House of Lords had held in those cases that conditions must be reasonable in principle and detail to be upheld. Here, the council was arguing that the conditions imposed effectively deprived them of their existing rights in the site, without compensation being payable. The court was of the opinion that the Secretary of State's decision had been wrong in law. The proposition that the condition imposed had been unacceptable in principle and detail was not accepted; it 'would not be compatible with a continuance of all the previous activities and all the existing work on the applicant's land or adjoining land'. The case was therefore remitted to the Secretary of State to be reconsidered.

Established-Use Certificates

Where land has been used without planning permission since 1963 or earlier a person having an interest in the land may apply to the planning authority for an established-use certificate which certifies that the particular use claimed has become established. The grant of the certificate thus means that the use to which the land is put cannot be challenged by an enforcement notice. If the certificate is refused the applicant may appeal to the Secretary of State, who must afford both applicant and planning authority an opportunity of being heard if either of them so desire.

The planning authority may issue an established-use certificate only where:

(i) the use began before the beginning of 1964 without planning permission and has continued since 1963, or

(ii) the use began before the beginning of 1964 under a planning permission granted subject to conditions or limitations which have never been complied with or have not been complied with since the end of 1963, or

(iii) the use began after the end of 1964 as the result of a change of use not requiring planning permission and there has been, since the end of 1963, no change of use requiring planning permission.

Stop Notices

A stop notice may be served by a local planning authority in conjunction with an enforcement notice. A stop notice prohibits the carrying out or continuing of specified operations on the land which are alleged to be in breach of planning control. The stop notice remains in force until the enforcement notice takes effect or is withdrawn or quashed. Breach of a stop notice may render the person responsible liable on summary conviction to a fine not exceeding £400.

There is no appeal against a stop notice, but planning authorities do not use them too freely because there is a compensation provision: where there is loss sustained as a result of the suspension of operations due to service of an enforcement notice, compensation for that loss may be claimed where it is shown that the enforcement notice was quashed on account of technical errors or grounds indicating that service of a stop notice was not justified, as it may where the stop notice is withdrawn.

PLANNING INQUIRIES

The Town and Country Planning (Inquiries Procedure) Rules 1969 regulate the procedure to be followed at local inquiries or hearings held in connection with planning applications referred or appeals taken to the Secretary of State for the Environment. The Rules also cover inquiries arising out of tree preservation orders, listed building consents, and hearings held in connection with the Town and Country Planning (Control of Advertisements) Regulations 1969.

No less than forty-two days' notice of the inquiry must be given by the

Secretary of State unless the appellant and the local planning authority agree to shorter notice.

An owner or agricultural tenant who must be notified of an application to develop his land by a person who is not the sole owner or tenant and who has made representations in connection with his application, will be notified of an inquiry into any appeal in connection with that application. Copies of any submissions to be made by the local planning authority at the inquiry will be provided for him and he will be entitled, as of right, to attend the inquiry.

The local planning authority's statement will include a copy of any direction given by the Secretary of State restricting the grant of the permission. Where an authority proposes to rely upon the views of a government department which opposes the application a statement of those views must also be included. Representatives of the departments in question will attend the inquiry at the request of the appellant not later than fourteen days before the inquiry. Where the Ministry of Agriculture has provided a technical appraisal of the agricultural considerations that are relevant to the proposed development the appellant may also request that a representative of the Ministry should attend.

The persons who are entitled to appear at an inquiry are:

(*a*) the applicant or appellant;

(*b*) the local planning authority;

(*c*) the council of the administrative county in which the land is situated (where there is a joint planning board);

(*d*) the council of the county district in which the land is situated;

(*e*) owners and agricultural tenants who are required to be notified of an application to develop the land and who have made representations in respect of the application (see page 130);

(*f*) the development corporation of a new town where the land is in an area designated as the site of a new town;

(*g*) any persons on whom the Secretary of State has required notice to be served;

(*h*) any persons who appear at the inquiry at the discretion of the person appointed to hold it.

The normal procedure at inquiries is for the inspector to open proceedings by stating the purpose of the inquiry, the parties enter appearance and the appellant opens his case – his advocate making an opening speech which summarises the appellant's case. In some cases the authority will open. Where the appellant's advocate has made his opening speech he will then call his witnesses. The inspector may require evidence to be given on oath but this is rarely done, and the rules of evidence applied are less formal than those pertaining in a court of law. Cross-examination of the witnesses may follow and re-examination by the appellant's advocate. The Inspector also may ask questions. Letters and documents relevant to the hearing are put in and the advocate for the respondent will then speak, and call his witnesses, with a concluding speech after the witnesses have been called. Other interested persons may then make their cases out, personally, or through advocates speaking for them.

The final speech is made by the appellant's advocate.

After the inquiry has been held a report and recommendations are submitted to the Secretary of State by the person responsible for holding the inquiry. If the Secretary of State disagrees with any recommendation made because he differs from the person making it on a finding of fact, or because he receives new evidence – including expert opinion on a matter of fact – or because he takes into consideration any new issue of fact he must not immediately reach a decision at variance with the recommendation. He must first notify the appellant, the local planning authority and any other persons entitled to be notified of the appeal who appeared at the inquiry of the situation. He must give them the opportunity to make further representations or to have the inquiry reopened.

In planning inquiries the parties are usually expected to bear their own costs but costs may be awarded where one of the parties has behaved unreasonably in the circumstances applying. Such awards are made only in exceptional situations.

Examination in Public of Structure Plans

Section 9 of the 1971 Act introduced a new method of dealing with objections to structure plans – the examination in public, which is designed to replace the public inquiry based on the formal hearing of objections.

The examination is conducted by an independent chairman and a panel, instead of a single inspector and is designed to investigate those matters arising on structure plans which the Secretary of State selects as calling for examination in public. The examination is conducted by way of a 'probing discussion' which covers not only arguments which are critical of the plan but also representations supporting it. It thus replaces the formalised procedures of the traditional inquiry into objections.

Selection of Matters for Examination. The Secretary of State's selection of matters for public examination will be based:

(a) on the structure plan – involving such issues as the future level and distribution of population and employment, policies and proposals for employment housing and transportation, major features of the plan, the implications of the plan for the area, and the availability of resources for major proposals;

(b) on the local planning authority's statement about publicity and public participation and consultation; and

(c) on objections and representations made on the plan as submitted.

The selection of matters helps to point to the authorities, organisations and individuals who should be invited to attend and take part. In selecting participants in the examination in public the Secretary of State will use as a basic criterion the effectiveness of the contribution which the parties can be expected to make to the discussion.

The Examination. Normally the examination in public will open from six to eight months after submission of the structure plan, and will last for three to six weeks. At a Preliminary Session discussions of an informal nature will be used to indicate the way in which the examination will be conducted. Thereafter a 'probing discussion' is led by the chairman and other panel members with the local planning authority and other participants, the aim being to secure a satisfactory examination of those matters selected so that the Secretary of State can obtain the further advice he needs before reaching a decision on the plan as a whole. Particular attention is paid to alternative proposals.

The intention behind the arrangements is to ensure informality and intensive discussion. Documents relevant to the examination are available before the meeting with transcripts available as it proceeds. Known material need not be rehearsed, therefore; the examination can concentrate on discussion.

Participants may be accompanied by professional or other advisers and advocates. A government department may be represented, to explain the department's views about the policies and proposals in the plan and give appropriate information.

Report. After conclusion of the examination in public the chairman will send the panel's report to the Secretary of State. It will be an assessment of the selected matters in the light of the discussion at the examination and it will include recommendations.

If new information comes to the Secretary of State it is published; if he proposes to make formal modifications to the structure plan they are advertised and an opportunity given for objections and representations to be made. These will be considered before a final decision is made.

The approved plan, the reasoned decision letter (which forms part of the plan) and the panel's report are all published and made available for inspection.

Local Plans. It should be re-emphasised that this procedure applies to structure plans. *Local* plans which are prepared by the local planning authority may also be faced with objections – but these objections and representations will be dealt with at a public inquiry held by an inspector appointed by the Secretary of State. The local planning authority will consider the inspector's report and adopt the plan with or without modification to meet objections to the plan. Modifications must be advertised and objections and representations to them must be considered. The Secretary of State has the power to direct that a particular local plan shall be submitted to him for his approval.

DETERMINATION OF PLANNING APPEALS BY INSPECTORS

Schedule 9 to the 1971 Act contains provisions whereby the Secretary of State may prescribe certain classes of planning appeals which may be determined by a departmental inspector rather than by himself. Regulations made under the Act[10] set out those classes of appeal which may be so determined; in general terms they are those appeals which are concerned with purely local issues. They include the following appeals:

    (a) as to the erection, enlargement or alteration of sixty dwellings or less;

    (b) as to residential development of not more than $4 \cdot 94$ acres of land where the number of dwellings is not stated;

    (c) as to certain developments of a non-residential character subject to limits of maximum floor area (500 square metres) and site area (8000 square metres);

    (d) formation, laying out or widening of a means of access;

(*e*) as to the change of use of buildings to any of the purposes noted in (*a*) and(*c*) above;

(*f*) as to change of use of land not exceeding 4000 square metres in area to use for the storage of materials (excluding scrap iron, refuse or waste), car-parking or the display and sale of motor-vehicles.

While appeals in these particular cases may be determined by an inspector there are some circumstances where they will nevertheless be subject to a decision of the Secretary of State. If they have been the subject of a Ministerial directive that permission should not be granted, or, if granted, they should be subject to conditions they are excepted from the general provision and must be decided upon by the Secretary of State. Similarly, appeals in these categories will be decided by him where the appellant is the local planning authority or a statutory undertaker; where the local planning authority has refused permission or granted it subject to conditions because of views expressed by a government department or by a new towns corporation; or where another appeal (which does not fall within the classes transferred for decision by inspectors) or an application or order relating to the same development or the same land is concurrently being considered by the Secretary of State.

Additionally, as a recognition of the special problems arising in London, where proposals relate to the building of hotels or the conversion of dwelling-houses to hotel use, appeals relating to hotel development in London are excluded from the transferred classes by a direction from the Secretary of State, who decides such matters himself.

LISTED BUILDINGS

Under the Town and Country Planning Acts the Secretary of State for the Environment and local planning authorities have powers to control the demolition, extension or alteration of buildings of special architectural or historic interest. Before the Act of 1968 was promulgated local planning authorities who wished to preserve such buildings could do so by making building-preservation orders but Part V of the 1968 Act introduced a new procedure whereby building-preservation orders were abolished and in their place equivalent protection was given to all 'listed buildings' whether they were the subject of a building-preservation order or not.

The Listing of Buildings

The provisions of the 1968 Act were consolidated in the Act of 1971; a duty is placed upon the Secretary of State to compile a list, after consultation with appropriate persons or bodies, of buildings which are of special architectural or historic interest, or to approve, with or without modification, lists compiled by other bodies. In considering whether to list a building the Secretary of State may take into account the building itself and any respect in which its exterior contributes to the architectural or historic interest of any group of buildings of which it forms part, or the desirability of preserving any man-made object or structure fixed to the building or comprised within its curtilage.

In England and Wales a copy of the relevant part of any list must be deposited with the council of the county borough, London borough or county district in whose area the buildings are situated (and with the local planning authority if the council for the area is not the planning authority). The council in question will then serve a notice on every owner and occupier of each listed building stating that it has been included in the list.

Listed Building Consents

It is an offence to demolish a listed building or to alter or extend it in a way that would affect its character as a building of special architectural or historic interest unless the work has been authorised by a 'listed building consent' issued by the local planning authority or the Secretary of State. In the case of demolition, notice must also be given to the Royal Commission on Historic Monuments in England or the Royal Commission on Ancient Monuments in Wales and Monmouthshire.

The consent may have attached to it conditions relating to the preservation of particular features of the building, the making good of any damage caused by the works or the reconstruction of the building with the use of original materials so far as is practicable and with such alterations of the interior as may be specified.

Where it is proposed to demolish the building and redevelop the site listed building consent must be obtained in addition to planning permission for the new building, but where a listed building is to be altered or extended in a way which would affect its character, specific planning permission for the proposed works may operate also as a listed building consent.

The procedure for applying for listed building consent is set out in the Town and Country Planning (Listed Buildings and Buildings in Conservation Areas) Regulations 1972; it is similar to that for planning permission, but the Secretary of State must be notified of an application to demolish so that he may decide whether or not to call in the application for determination. The local planning authority must give local publicity to applications and carry out consultations directed by the Secretary of State.

If an application is refused or a consent granted subject to conditions by the local planning authority there is a right of appeal to the Secretary of State. If an owner claims that the refusal, or the conditions imposed, have made the land incapable of reasonably beneficial use he may serve a purchase notice on the appropriate local authority, or as an alternative, in certain limited circumstances, he may claim compensation.

Conservation Areas

Under section 8 of the Town and Country Planning (Amendment) Act 1972 local planning authorities could exercise demolition control over unlisted buildings in conservation areas in certain circumstances. The new section 277A of the Town and Country Amenities Act 1974 made listed building control of application to *all* buildings within conservation areas (with certain exceptions, see above, page 138). The result is that anyone wishing to demolish a building in a conservation area must apply for listed building consent to the local planning authority, separately, or as part of an application for planning permission for redevelopment of the site. The local planning authority must pay regard to the importance of the building to the character and appearance of any part of the conservation area in assessing whether consent should be granted.

Demolition consent is granted as part of planning permission only where the permission specifically states that it is included. Authorities granting outline planning permission are likely to exclude such demolition consent in giving the permission.

Circular 147/74 of the Department of the Environment pointed out that consent to demolish should be given only where there are acceptable and detailed plans for redevelopment so that unsightly gaps in conservation areas should not be allowed to appear. Local authorities seeking consent to demolish a building in a conservation area must make application direct to the Secretary of State.

Since section 290(1) defines 'building' as any part of a building it is likely that demolition of part of a building would be regarded as demolition of a building for the purposes of section 277A.

Building Preservation Notices

Emergency controls are available in the building-preservation notice system. If a non-listed building is regarded as of special architectural or historic interest, and the planning authority considers that it is in danger of demolition or alteration affecting its special character, it may serve a building-preservation notice on the owner or occupier. In emergency cases the notice may be affixed conspicuously to the building itself.

The notice states that the planning authority has requested the Secretary of State to consider including the building in the list. The notice will remain in force for six months unless before the end of that period the Secretary of State either lists the building or notifies the planning authority that he does not intend to list it. While it is in force the building-preservation notice has the effect of imposing immediate control so as to make the building as protected as though it were a listed building.

Listed Building Enforcement Notices

Where work has been undertaken on a listed building without consent, or without compliance with conditions attached to a consent, local planning authorities and, in appropriate cases, the Secretary of State, may serve an enforcement notice. This will require the building to be restored to its former state, or to be brought up to the state it would have been in if the conditions had been complied with, within a specified period.

A right of appeal against the notice lies to the Secretary of State. Failure to comply with the notice is an offence punishable by a fine but the planning authority (or the Secretary of State where he served the notice) is also empowered to enter upon the land and take such steps as are specified in the enforcement notice, with expenses being recovered from the owner of the property.

Urgent Repair of Unoccupied Buildings

By the (amended)[11] section 101 of the 1971 Act:

(a) a local authority can execute works for the preservation of an unoccupied listed building if it appears that the works are urgently necessary; and (*b*) the Secretary of State may execute such works, and in the case of unlisted buildings in conservation areas where it is important to preserve them for the maintenance of the character or appearance of the area, may direct that such works of preservation be undertaken.

The owner of the building must be given seven days' notice in writing; he may be required to pay the expenses incurred unless within twenty-eight days he successfully represents to the Secretary of State that the sum is unreasonable, or to pay it would cause him hardship, or that some or all of the works were unnecessary for preservation of the building.

Repairs Notice

If the planning authority considers that a listed building is not being properly preserved it may serve upon the owner a repairs notice which specifies works considered necessary to preserve the building. If the work is not carried out the planning authority, with the consent of the Secretary of State, may acquire compulsorily the building in question. Compensation for the acquisition may be reduced to 'minimum compensation' where it can be shown that the building has been neglected deliberately, in order that it might be demolished and redevelopment carried on thereafter.

The repairs notice must give the owner at least two months' notice to carry out the works specified.

Grants

The introduction of the general grant in 1958 meant that exchequer grants in respect of planning ceased to be payable but there are certain exceptions to the general rule.

(1) By section 250 of the 1971 Act and the Town and Country Planning (Grants) Regulations 1968 (as amended) a grant is payable in respect of the acquisition, clearing and preliminary development of land acquired for the redevelopment as a whole of any area whether or not defined as an area of comprehensive development, or for the relocation of population or industry, or the replacement of public space, in the course of such development.

(2) By section 10 of the Town and Country Planning (Amendment) Act 1972 the Secretary of State can make grants and loans for the preservation or enhancement of character or appearance of conservation areas.

(3) By section 253 of the 1971 Act the Secretary of State may make grants to assist establishments engaged in research and education connected with the planning and design of the physical environment.

AMENITIES CONTROL

Some reference has already been made to various statutory provisions that empower local authorities to take steps for the preservation of amenities: cases in point are powers available in conservation areas and powers and duties concerning the deposit of waste. Further powers exist in relation to trees and waste land.

Preservation of Trees

Local authority powers in this matter are governed by sections 60 to 62 of the 1971 Act, as amended by the Town and Country Amenities Act 1974; where, however, a forestry dedication agreement is in force or where the Forestry Commissioners have made a grant under the Forestry Act 1967 that Act also has application.

The provisions give powers, in the interests of amenity, to local authorities to make tree-preservation orders. These are designed to control the felling, lopping or wilful destruction of individual trees, groups of trees or woodlands. The order may provide for the replanting of woodland after forestry operations; alternatively the local authority may impose a planning condition requiring replanting on any consent to fell that it gives in pursuance of an order.

There is a general requirement to replace any tree which is protected by an order other than a woodland tree which falls, or is felled without express consent. The requirement may be enforced by the service upon the owner of the land of a notice; the planning authority must serve this notice within four years of the failure to replant.

If an application for consent to fell or lop a protected tree is refused by the planning authority appeal may be made to the Secretary of State and compensation may be payable. The Town and Country Planning (Tree Preservation Order) Regulations 1969 prescribe the procedure which must be followed in the making of an order, including provision for an unopposed order to be confirmed by the authority making the order.

Where the order is opposed it is subject to confirmation by the Secretary of State, but an authority may make an order immediately operative pending confirmation or otherwise by special direction in the order.

Where a tree-preservation order is contravened the person summarily convicted of the offence may be fined up to £400 or twice the value of the tree, whichever is the greater, if the tree is cut down, uprooted, wilfully destroyed or damaged. For other offences the maximum fine is £200 with an additional daily penalty of up to £5 where the offence continues.

All trees in conservation areas are protected, even if no preservation orders have been made in respect of them[12] but certain defences are available to persons charged with an offence under the section (section 8 of the 1974 Act, amending section 61 of the 1971 Act). It is a defence to show that the person charged:

(*a*) served notice of his intention to do the act in question, identifying the tree, on the district or London borough council in whose area the tree is situated; and

(*b*) that he did the act
   (i) with the consent of the local planning authority, or
   (ii) after the end of six weeks from the date of notice but before the end of two years from that date.

The district and London borough councils are under a duty to compile and keep available for public inspection, free of charge, a register of particulars of notices affecting trees in their areas. Where a tree is removed, uprooted or destroyed it is the duty of the owner of the land to replace it unless the local planning authority, on his application, releases him from the obligation.

Schemes of Enhancement

Section 277B of the 1971 Act (as amended by the Act of 1974) places a duty on local authorities, at such time as the Secretary of State may direct, to formulate and publish proposals for the preservation and enhancement of conservation areas and to submit them for consideration to a local public meeting. The authorities should seek the advice and views of local residents and amenity groups in formulating their schemes and should also invite such people to any meetings held to obtain comment and advice.

Waste Land

Section 65 of the 1971 Act states that where the amenity of an area is seriously injured by the condition of 'open land' the local planning authority may serve a notice upon the owner and occupier requiring clearance of the area. In *Stephens v. Cuckfield Rural District Council*(1960) the Court of Appeal held that whether land was properly open land was a question of fact to be determined by the particular circumstances. It did not necessarily include unbuilt land not surrounded by other buildings, nor was it necessarily excluded because it was surrounded by a fence.

The local authority may serve the notice even where the condition of the land complained of is the result of an existing use. Appeal lies against a notice to the magistrates' court. The powers of enforcement are similar to those which apply in relation to service of an enforcement notice.

CONTROL OF ADVERTISING

Under the Town and Country Planning Acts the Secretary of State for the Environment may make regulations to control the display of advertisements in the interests of amenity and public safety. By 'advertisement' is meant any word, letter, model, sign, placard, board, notice, devise or representation, illuminated or not, in the nature of and employed wholly or in part for the purposes of advertisement, announcement or direction. The definition excludes things used as memorials or railway signals but extends to any hoarding used or adapted for use to display advertisements.

In general an advertisement may not be displayed unless consent is given by the regulations[13] themselves, or by express consent of the local planning authority, or by the Secretary of State.

Excepted Advertisements

Certain advertisements are excepted from the regulations. They are:
- (a) advertisements displayed on enclosed land and not readily visible to the public;
- (b) advertisements displayed within a building (other than in certain special cases – see page 145);
- (c) advertisements displayed on or in a vehicle (except for periods where it is used primarily as an advertisement display);
- (d) advertisements incorporated in the fabric of a building (but not one used principally for display);

(*e*) advertisements displayed on articles for sale, or their packages, containers or dispensers, where they refer to the articles, are not illuminated, and do not exceed 0·1 square metre in area.

Standard Conditions

Local authorities must have regard only to amenity or public safety and cannot impose limitations on the subject-matter, content or design of advertisements except that in the case of a particular advertisement they may have regard to the effect it will have on amenity or public safety.

Otherwise standard conditions are prescribed which call for conformity:

(*a*) advertisements and the land used for their display must be kept clean and tidy;

(*b*) structures such as hoardings must be maintained in a safe condition;

(*c*) removal must be carried out to the satisfaction of the local authority.

Permitted Advertisements

Advertisements which were displayed on 1 August 1948 and advertisements which continue to be displayed after express consent has expired (unless the express consent contained a condition to the contrary) and renewal has not been refused are permitted by the regulations. Similarly, election notices, statutory advertisements and traffic signs are permitted under the regulations. Otherwise certain specified classes are laid down where consent is deemed to be granted for advertising display purposes. They are as follows:

(i) Functional advertisements of local authorities, statutory undertakers and public transport undertakers;

(ii) advertisements relating to the premises on which they are displayed, for the purpose of identification or direction, or warning; or which relate to a profession, business or trade or to religious, educational and other specified institutions, including hotels, inns, clubs and hostels;

(iii) advertisements of a temporary nature, such as those advertising the sale of property, or of goods or livestock, and those which are displayed on land on which building or similar works is being carried on;

(iv) advertisements on business premises wholly relating to the business, the goods sold and services provided, and the name and qualifications of the owner;

(v) advertisements on the forecourt of business premises;

(vi) flag advertisements.

With the exception of the first of the classes noted above the regulations prescribe maximum sizes for advertisements and if an advertisement exceeds the size laid down express consent must be obtained from the local planning authority. Restrictions are placed also upon the advertisements as far as illumination is concerned and those which are noted in (iii) above must not be displayed more than twenty-eight days before the commencement of the event to which they relate and they must be removed within fourteen days after its conclusion.

The local planning authority is still entitled to serve a notice requiring discontinuance of the display even though they are deemed to have consent; equally, the authority may grant express consent without imposing the conditions that apply in respect of the permitted advertisements.

The Secretary of State has the power to exclude, on his own initiative or on application from the local authority, any area, or any particular case, from the provisions noted above and he may direct that in that area or in that case advertisements of the specified classes shall require express consent.

Express Consent

Where it is desired to display an advertisement which is not within the classes of permitted advertisements an application for consent must be made to the local planning authority. The local planning authority have a duty to consult various bodies likely to be affected by the display and in reaching a decision must have regard to the interests of amenity, taking into account the general characteristics of the locality, the presence of historical and architectural features, public safety and so on. The standard conditions already noted will apply, but others may be imposed in addition by the authority. A consent runs for five years though the Secretary of State may give a consent for a longer period. Where less than five years is consented to it is deemed to be a condition attached to the consent. Applications for renewal of a consent may be made within a period of six months before its expiry.

The local planning authority must give reasons for its decision when it refuses consent, or grants it subject to conditions, or grants it for a period less than five years. An appeal lies from the decision in these cases to the Secretary of State, whose decision on the matter is final. He must give the parties an opportunity to be heard unless he considers that he is already sufficiently informed.

Revocation or modification of the consent by the authority is possible at any time before the display is begun. The order is not effective until confirmation by the Secretary of State has been made; the parties must have had an opportunity to be heard by the person appointed by the Secretary of State for that purpose. Where there is any loss directly attributable to the revocation or modification compensation may be payable, but in any case not to cover depreciation in the value of the land.

Special Kinds of Advertisements

Certain kinds of 'advertisement' are given special treatment under the Act.

(1) Election notices, statutory advertisements and traffic signs may be displayed without express consent, though election notices must be removed within fourteen days after the poll and statutory advertisements must be removed within a reasonable time after the requirements have been satisfied.

(2) Local planning authorities may display advertisements on land for which they are the planning authority, but in areas of special control (see below, p. 148) they may only display advertisements for which they could themselves give consent.

(3) Consent may be granted for the temporary display on unspecified sites of advertisements for travelling circuses and fairs, by the local planning authority. They must not be put up more than fourteen days before the first performance or opening and must be removed within seven days of the last performance or closing. There are also restrictions on the size of such advertisements.

(4) Illuminated advertisements within buildings and visible from outside, those within one metre of an external door, window or other opening through which they are visible from outside and all advertisements displayed in buildings used principally for the display of such advertisements which are visible from outside are subject to certain limited controls.

Areas of Special Control

Local planning authorities are required to review at least once every five years the use of their power to define areas of special control. Over one-third of Great Britain is now subject to special control. In such areas, which may be defined as open countryside and places requiring special protection on grounds of amenity and designated as such by order of the planning authority, the display of advertising is governed by special rules.

The basic principle is that in areas of special control no advertisements may be displayed subject to certain exceptions. They include those advertisements which fall into the specified classes already mentioned, but with further restrictions regarding height and size of lettering; election notices, statutory advertisements and traffic signs; advertisements for travelling circuses and fairs, and advertisements which are inside buildings but visible outside. In addition the local planning authority may give express consent for advertisements relating to local activities, for announcement or direction in respect of buildings or land in the area and for advertisements necessary for public safety.

An area cannot be considered as a special control area unless it is rural in nature or unless the Secretary of State considers that it requires special protection on the ground of amenity. An order by the local planning authority defining a special control area does not become effective until it is confirmed by the Secretary of State. The authority must have consulted interested bodies and the regulations provide that a local public inquiry should be held where objections to the order are lodged.

Formerly an area could not be considered as a special control area unless it was rural in nature. The relevant section of the 1971 Act, section 63, was amended by section 3 of the Town and Country Amenities Act 1974 so as to enable the Secretary of State, in making regulations for advertisement control, to make provisions not only in rural areas, but also *any* areas which appear to him to require special protection on grounds of amenity. Special provision of this kind may also be made in respect of conservation areas – the objective being that local authorities will in future be able to exercise control in a flexible and sensitive manner.

Enforcement Procedures

The enforcement provisions relating to advertisement control are found in section 109 of the 1971 Act and the Town and Country Planning (Control of Advertisements) Regulations 1969.

The provisions of the regulations are enforced by way of prosecution in courts of summary jurisdiction. Where a person has contravened the regulations he may be prosecuted and is liable on summary conviction to a fine not exceeding £100. For every day that the offence continues the court may impose an additional daily penalty of £5.

Under section 109 persons who advertise goods in contravention of the provisions are liable; but, equally, the occupier and owner of the land on which the advertisement appears will also be liable, together with the person who set up the display. It is a good defence, however, to show that where the person charged under this section was not directly responsible for the display he did not know of or consent to the display in breach of the regulations.

Where the advertisement is one for which consent is deemed to be granted under the regulations (see below) the local authority must first serve a discontinuance order. When the order takes effect it will become enforceable in a court of summary jurisdiction.

Flyposting

The posting of bills or notices on land or buildings without knowledge or permission of the owner or occupier is forbidden by the regulations, which state that it is a condition of consent, whether expressly imposed or not, that the owner's consent (or that of someone entitled to give such consent) must be obtained before an advertisement can be displayed on his land or buildings. The only exception is for such statutory notices as are required to be displayed although no permission has been obtained.

APPROPRIATION, DISPOSAL AND DEVELOPMENT

The powers of local authorities to acquire land by way of compulsory purchase are dealt with in the next chapter. The matter of appropriation may more conveniently be dealt with here.

Appropriation

By section 122 of the Local Government Act 1972 a local authority may appropriate land held for one purpose to another statutory purpose. But though this is the general rule it is subject to certain exceptions.

(1) Open space and common land may not be appropriated under this section if it exceeds an area of 209 square metres appropriation is then possible only under section 121 of the Town and Country Planning Act 1971, which involves special parliamentary procedure. Exceptionally it can be dispensed with if equally advantageous land is provided in exchange, or where the land is required to widen or drain a highway and the Secretary of State is satisfied that exchanged land is not necessary.

(2) In the case of first appropriation of land acquired under compulsory powers, or under the threat of compulsory powers within ten years before the date of the proposed appropriation, the consent of the Secretary of State is required.

As far as land held for planning purposes is concerned, however, by section 122 of the 1971 Act such land may be appropriated for other purposes.

Disposal

The general rule, laid down in section 123 of the Local Government Act 1972, is that a local authority may dispose of any of its land. But, again, there are exceptions to this rule:

(1) Public trust land exceeding 209 square metres in area cannot be disposed of under section 123.

(2) If it is intended to dispose of the land at less than the best rent that can reasonably be obtained the consent of the appropriate Minister must be obtained. This, however, does not apply in the case of a short tenancy.

(3) If the land is open space within the meaning of the Town and Country Planning Act 1971, or if the land was acquired under compulsory purchase powers, or if the land was acquired under the shadow of compulsory purchase powers within ten years and has not subsequently been appropriated, ministerial consent is required.

Development

By section 124 of the 1971 Act an authority may construct or carry out any building or work on land acquired or appropriated for planning purposes. This power cannot be relied upon to carry out work or building for which express statutory power exists under some other enactment.

Sections 2 to 5 of the Local Authorities (Land) Act 1963 give further development powers to local authorities, whereby they may erect buildings and construct and carry out works on land with the consent of the Secretary of State and for the benefit or improvement of the area. Under these sections on disposal of land the authority is empowered to lend money to the purchaser or lessee of the land in order to enable him to erect buildings on that land, and garages may be erected and buildings may be converted into garages. Money may also be lent in pursuance of building agreements.

THE DOBRY REPORT

The preparation of development plans was considered by the Planning Advisory Group in 1965: the result was the Town and Country Planning Act 1968, Part I (now Part II of the 1971 Act as amended). Development control and the system of appeals was not dealt with; Mr G. Dobry, Q.C., was appointed to consider these aspects, with an advisory group, and produced an Interim Report in 1974 (*Review of the Development Control System*). In September 1974 a further report appeared: *Control of Demolition.*

Demolition of listed buildings has been illegal since 1968, unless listed building consent is obtained. Conservation area buildings were protected by section 8 of the Town and Country Planning (Amendment) Act 1972 and the new section 277A of the 1971 Act (introduced by section 1 of the Town and Country Amenities Act 1974)..Exceptions were listed in para. 15 of Circular 147/74 of the Department of the Environment (see above, page 139). The Dobry Report on Control of Demolition now advocates that all demolition should require listed building consent or be specifically authorised by a planning permission.

Mr Dobry was impressed by the arguments of the local authority associations who drew attention to neglected sites which became rubbish dumps. There was also the problem of developers who used such situations to force the hand of planning authorities. On the other hand the Report mentions arguments to the contrary – diminution of individual rights, extra burden of work on planning authorities, and enforcement problems: demolition can often be carried out at speed, before the authority knows what is happening. The Report suggests, nevertheless, that:

 (i) demolition without permission should be an offence;
 (ii) powers should be given to planning authorities to make compulsory purchase orders by summary procedures with limited compensation;
 (iii) planning authorities should be given a limited power to order restoration, or in default restore the building themselves at the owner's expense.

The first two of these would certainly have deterrent value. The Report suggests that hardship might arise where permission to demolish is refused but this could be solved by the purchase-notice procedure.

The favour with which the Report has generally been received would suggest that its implementation may well be undertaken in the near future, with consequent further planning legislation being enacted.

The Final Report produced by Mr Dobry contained 161 recommendations. It suggested that the system of control of development is basically sound and recommended the better practices already in force in some authorities – for instance, more regular planning meetings – should be undertaken by all. The most radical change suggested was that planning applications should be divided into two categories. Class A should comprise all simple applications which comply with an approved development plan, or which only just exceed tolerances in the General Development Plan, and approval of reserved matters on an outline which was Class A. All others, which would be regarded as 'controversial', would be Class B. Class A applications would follow a swift procedure, a decision to be reached within thirty-five to forty-two days, otherwise permission would be deemed to be given. For Class B applications there would be greater publicity and less speed in dealing with the application.

The appeals system also, it is suggested, should be streamlined, with simple appeals being dealt with by the inspector giving an oral decision with written confirmation later. And while either side at present can demand a public inquiry, the Dobry Report suggests that the Secretary of State should be allowed to insist on written representations instead.

The report also deals with enforcement procedures, and argues that 'stop notices' should be used more often and extended to changes of use as well as the carrying out of operations. It also recommends that planning authorities should be allowed to require the occupier to give factual information regarding his use of the land so that more accurate enforcement notices can be prepared by the planning authorities.

NOTE

The Government in fact rejected almost all the main recommendations of the Dobry Report. In particular, the proposed division of planning applications into major and minor, and the suggestion that demolition of all buildings should be subject to planning control were rejected.

REFERENCES

1. As amended by the Town and Country Planning (Amendment) Act 1972.
2. A Code of Practice for proceedings in the public examination is published by the Department of the Environment (1973).
3. Of which not more than fourteen days may be used for motor or motor-cycle racing or the holding of markets.
4. *Pyx Granite Co. Ltd v. Minister of Housing and Local Government*, [1958] 1 All E.R. 625; *Fawcett Properties Ltd v. Buckingham County Council*, [1960] 3 All E.R. 503.
5. *Pyx Granite Co. Ltd v. Ministry of Housing and Local Government*, [1958] 1 Q.B. 554, p. 572.
6. A certificate is not required in development areas defined in the Development Areas Order 1966 and the Town and Country Planning (Industrial Development Certificates) Regulations 1972, but in some areas the exemption limit is 10,000 square feet and in others 15,000 square feet.
7. The full list appears in section 242.
8. Under section 246 of the 1971 Act.
9. Which states a local planning authority may grant planning permission 'subject to conditions as they think fit'; and by section 30(1)(a) may do so 'for regulating the development or use of land.' See also *Hall & Co. Ltd v. Shoreham-by-Sea Urban District Council*, [1964] 1 All E.R. 1; *Prosser v. Minister of Housing and Local Government* (1968), 67 L.G.R. 109; and *Minister of Housing and Local Government v. Hartnell*, [1965] 1 All E.R. 490.
10. Town and Country Planning (Determination of Appeals by Appointed Persons) (Prescribed Classes) Regulations 1972.
11. By section 5(1) of the Town and Country Amenities Act 1974.
12. Certain trees may be exempted by regulations to be published by the Secretary of State; section 61A(4) of the 1971 Act.
13. Town and Country Planning (Control of Advertisements) Regulations 1969, as amended.

7

Compulsory Purchase

Sections 120 and 124 of the Local Government Act 1972 gives power to local authorities (principal authorities, parish councils and community councils) to enter into agreements to acquire land by purchase, lease or exchange for the purpose of any of their functions, or for the benefit, improvement or development of their areas. In such cases the land may be within or outside the area of the authority. Section 119 of the Town and Country Planning Act 1971 gives an almost equally widely-drawn power to purchase by agreement – the section states that a principal council may purchase land for the development or re-development of any adjacent land, and the council may buy land for a purpose which it is necessary to achieve in the interests of the proper planning of an area in which the land is situated.

In addition to such general powers, however, there are certain specific powers falling to the local authorities, and it is often the case that the authorities rely more on these specific powers to purchase land by agreement rather than on the general powers even though the latter may be more convenient to use. Thus section 97 of the Housing Act 1957 enables housing authorities to acquire land by agreement and section 9 of the Open Spaces Act 1906 gives them power to buy land for use as an open space or burial-ground.

Where such powers are brought into operation, either specific or general, the vendor and the purchaser reach an agreed price, with the authority obtaining Ministerial consent where necessary for the raising of any loan it requires in order to buy the land. The Minister normally relies upon the district valuer's report in such cases to satisfy himself as to the price to be paid. Approval is also necessary where a grant is to be paid. Where the authority has statutory powers to buy the land compulsorily, but decides to do it by agreement, the Minister will approve the price if it is calculated on the basis of compensation for a compulsory purchase as certified by the district valuer. If compulsory purchase powers are not available the purchase price for the land must not be greater than the full market value as certified by the district valuer.

But these provisions relate generally to purchase by agreement. The specific power mentioned above, under section 97 of the Housing Act 1957, also gives authorities power to buy land compulsorily for the provision of housing accommodation. It is one of many.

STATUTORY POWERS

The power to purchase land compulsorily is the creature of statute. In the nineteenth century private Bills were necessary to achieve such objects until the Land Clauses Consolidation Act 1845 made the situation easier. Its provisions were eventually consolidated in the Compulsory Purchase Act 1965, but this has not dried up the flow of private Acts entirely: local authorities still, from time to time, make use of this procedure to obtain the powers they desire.

The acquisition of compulsory purchase powers by provisional order became possible as a result of the Public Health Act 1875, whereby an authority could present a petition to the Local Government Board which, after a public inquiry, could make a provisional order granting the powers. The order required confirmation by Parliament. In the early twentieth century the procedure was smoothed by several Acts which enabled the confirmation to be made by a Minister rather than by Parliament, and this is the present position in most cases. Many statutory powers may be exercised by authorities making compulsory purchase orders, and these orders become effective when confirmed by the appropriate Minister.

General Powers

We may take as an example of the procedure involved the general powers continued in section 121 of the Local Government Act 1972. The councils of counties, county boroughs, and county districts – and in London the Greater London Council, the Common Council and the London Borough Councils – may acquire land by compulsory purchase for development and re-development and lease it to private developers and may undertake development themselves. The principal authorities, in effect, may acquire land compulsorily for any of their functions, and district councils can exercise compulsory powers to purchase land on behalf of parish or community councils which are unable to acquire land on reasonable terms (provided they have legal authority to purchase such land). District councils must hold public inquiries where such purchases are contemplated.

The powers laid down in section 121 cannot be used to acquire land under section 120, for the 'benefit, improvement or development of the area'; nor can they be used for functions under the Local Authorities (Land) Act 1963. It has already been noted that some Acts give authorities power to acquire land by agreement – section 9 of the Open Spaces Act 1906 was the example given. The section 121 powers cannot be used for such purposes as these.

But what if land is required for more than one purpose? It may then be included in a compulsory acquisition; equally, two or more authorities may join forces in a compulsory acquisition, with one council acting for the others. The Minister or Ministers concerned are under no obligation to apportion as between purposes, or as between authorities.

A further example of general powers appears in section 112 of the Town and Country Planning Act 1971. Under this section the Secretary of State may authorise a principal council to acquire compulsorily any land in its area, provided he is satisfied as to certain matters. They are:

(*a*) that the land is required to secure or assist the treatment as a whole, by development, redevelopment or improvement, or partly by one and partly by another method, of the land or of any area in which the land is situated; or

(*b*) that it is expedient in the public interest that the land should be held together with land so required; or

(*c*) that the land is required for development or re-development or both, as a whole for the purpose of providing for the relocation of population or industry or the replacement of open space in the course of the redevelopment or improvement, or both, of another area as a whole; or

(*d*) that it is expedient to acquire the land immediately for a purpose which it is necessary to achieve in the interests of the proper planning of an area in which the land is situated.

Where the Secretary of State wishes to authorise an authority to acquire land within the area of another local authority he must first consult that other local authority.

Specific Powers

Specific powers of compulsory acquisition are found in a number of statutes. Thus, under the Highway Acts 1959 to 1971, highway authorities have power to acquire by compulsory purchase[1] land for a number of purposes, including:

  (i) to construct, improve or alter an existing highway;

  (ii) to prevent the erection of buildings detrimental to the view from the highway;

  (iii) to improve or develop the frontages to the highway;

  (iv) to provide new means of access from the highway to any premises;

  (v) to divert a navigable waterway for purposes of road construction, improvement or alteration;

  (vi) to provide service stations for trunk roads and special roads.

Compulsory purchases by local highway authorities in general require the approval of the Secretary of State. The Acts also prescribe distance limits which apply to the compulsory purchase of land for purposes such as those above. The distance limit is normally 200 metres from the middle of the highway or proposed highway, and 800 metres where the land is required for the provision of new means of access or a service area. No distance limits are prescribed for (v) above.

Other powers are found in, for instance:

(1) Housing Act 1957 – purchase for temporary accommodation of houses unfit for human habitation (sections 12 and 29); provision of housing accommodation (section 97); land comprised in or surrounded by or adjoining a clearance area (section 43(3)); land cleared in accordance with a clearance order but which owners have failed to develop (section 51);

(2) Caravan Sites and Control of Development Act 1960 – purchase of sites (section 24);

(3) Coast Protection Act 1949 – carrying out coast protection work (sections 14 and 27).

AUTHORISATION OF COMPULSORY ACQUISITION

Before an authority can exercise a statutory power to acquire land compulsorily in any particular case it must obtain a specific authorisation to do so. The procedural code is set out in the Acquisition of Land (Authorisation Procedures) Act 1946, although in the case of land acquired compulsorily under Part III of the Housing Act 1957 which deals with clearance areas a similar code, contained in the Act itself, applies.[2]

The Secretary of State's powers in this respect are laid down in section 112 of the Town and Country Planning Act 1971 (see above, p. 156). He may also acquire compulsorily any land necessary for the public service and may empower a local authority to acquire compulsorily a listed building in need of repair.

By the Compulsory Purchase of Land Regulations 1972 the authority must first of all make a compulsory purchase order in the prescribed form.

Compulsory Purchase Orders

The compulsory purchase order must describe by reference to a map the land to which it relates. It must also cite the statute on which the authority is relying in the exercise of the power.

The order must be submitted to the appropriate Minister for his confirmation. This will be the Minister who is empowered to authorise the purchase by the statute under which the land is acquired. Before submitting the order, however, the authority must publish in one or more local newspapers on two successive weeks a notice which states that the order is to be submitted for confirmation. It must also give details of the contents of the order and specify a time, not less than twenty-one days, within which objections may be made. Similar notices must be sent to owners, lessees and occupiers of the land in question, but not to tenants for a month or less.

If it is not practicable to find the names of owners lessees or occupiers the Minister may direct that the notice can be affixed to the land or delivered to some person on the premises. If no objections are raised, or if objections are made but withdrawn, the Minister may confirm the order with or without modifications.

Public Inquiries

If objections are raised, and relate to matters other than compensation, the Minister must hold a local public inquiry at which the objector and the acquiring authority may state their views. The procedure to be followed is laid down in the Compulsory Purchase by Local Authorities (Inquiries Procedure) Rules 1962 and is similar to that relating to planning inquiries (see page 132) except that the persons who will be notified are the 'statutory objectors' – that is, the persons entitled under the Acquisition of Land (Authorisation Procedures) Act 1946 to be served with notice of the making of the order and who have duly objected to its making, and any other persons who in the view of the Minister should be given the opportunity of being heard.

As far as notices generally are concerned it was held in *Grimley v. Minister of Housing and Local Government* (1971) that notices must be served on owners of land, but 'land' did not include an easement of support, so the owner of the dominant tenement in this instance had no right to receive notice.

Confirmation

When the Minister reaches his decision as to whether the compulsory purchase order should be confirmed or not he is acting in an administrative capacity. It follows that since his action is not of a judicial nature he may with impunity take into account matters other than those which have been raised at the public inquiry. In *Miller v. Minister of Health* (1946) the Minister took into account a letter which contained the views of government departments concerning a proposed compulsory purchase order. Though the letter had been written before the public inquiry commenced it had not been introduced into evidence at the inquiry. The court held that the Minister had not acted improperly: he was acting in an administrative capacity and, as such, considerations of policy could be taken into account when he reached his decision which was to be, what was best for the community.

By section 12 of the Tribunals and Inquiries Act 1971 the Minister must give reasons for his decision.

Persons Aggrieved

When the order has been confirmed notice of the confirmation must be published in one or more local newspapers and sent to those persons to whom notice was earlier given (or otherwise, where the Minister consents, is affixed to the land or delivered to a person on the premises). The operative date for the order is the date of first publication.

A person who is aggrieved by the order may challenge it in two ways only:

(i) on the ground that it is *ultra vires*, or
(ii) on the ground that there has been a failure to comply with some statutory requirement.

Persons aggrieved must use the proceedings established in the First Schedule to the 1946 Act; they have six weeks in which to apply to the High Court for quashing of the order, the six weeks to run from the date on which the order became operative.

Where the ground of complaint is that a statutory requirement was not fulfilled the court can quash the order only where it is satisfied that the interests of the applicant have been substantially prejudiced by the failure to observe the formalities. If the order is not challenged within the six weeks' period, it cannot thereafter be raised. But what if the aggrieved party was prevented from challenging within the period by some fraud? In *Anisminic Ltd v. Foreign Compensation Commission* (1967) it was held that an apparently regular order is protected even if it is made with improper motives for its motives are not apparent on its face. Some criticism was advanced in this case of the principle laid down in *Smith v. East Elloe Rural District Council* (1956) but the decision in *Smith* was later followed in *Routh v. Reading Corporation* (1970). The matter discussed in *Smith* was as follows.

The Acquisition of Land (Authorisation Procedures) Act 1946 provided, effectively, that:

(a) a person aggrieved by a compulsory purchase order may challenge it on the grounds that 'it is not empowered to be granted under this Act' or that 'any requirement of this Act . . . has not been complied with' by applying to the High Court within six weeks of notice of confirmation; and

(b) subject to the above a compulsory purchase order shall not be questioned 'in any legal proceedings whatsoever'.

Three of the judges in the House of Lords held that challenge on the ground of fraud was barred after the six weeks because of (b) above. Two judges dissented from this view. The seriousness of the variety of opinions expressed was such that Lord Denning M.R. held in *Webb v. Minister of Housing and Local Government* (1965) that the decision gave no clear guidance and should not be regarded as a binding authority. But in *Webb* a different point was in issue. An urban district council had made a scheme for building a sea-wall under their power as coast-protection authority. The scheme included a promenade behind the wall for which land was acquired compulsorily. But this land was not strictly required for coast *protection* so the compulsory purchase order was invalid – it was *ultra vires*. The council had certainly made untrue and misleading statements but the court considered these were the result of ineptitude rather than bad faith. Even so, Lord Denning had a point when he said, elsewhere[3]

No judgment of a court, no order of a Minister, can be allowed to stand if it has been obtained by fraud – fraud unravels everything.

But not, as the law stands, a compulsory purchase order confirmation where a challenge arises after the expiry of the six weeks' period.

Statutory Orders (Special Procedure) Acts

Under Acts of 1945 and 1965 special parliamentary procedures are applied in certain cases. Thus, where land

    (*a*) is owned by a local authority or statutory undertaker for the purposes of the undertaking, or is held inalienably by the National Trust; or

    (*b*) forms part of a common or open space; or

    (*c*) comprises an ancient monument or other object of archaeological interest,

special procedures apply. In the case of (*a*) the Minister cannot make a compulsory purchase order unless he first certifies that the land can be sold without serious detriment to the undertaking or can be replaced with other land without serious detriment. Special parliamentary procedure is applied to (*b*) unless the Minister certifies that equivalent land will be given in exchange, or that the land is required for road widening and the giving of other land in exchange is unnecessary.

Before the Minister issues a certificate he must give interested persons the opportunity to make representations to him.

A compulsory purchase order which affects (*c*) is subject to special parliamentary procedure unless the Secretary of State certifies that the authority acquiring the land has agreed to observe appropriate conditions as to the use of the land.

NOTICES TO TREAT

The Compulsory Purchase Act 1965 lays down the general rules of procedure for the steps to be taken after a compulsory purchase order has been made and confirmed. By section 5 of the Act the local authority is required, after confirmation of the order, to serve on all interested parties a notice stating that the authority has been authorised to acquire the land and is willing to treat for its purchase. The notice will also ask the persons interested in the land for details of their interests and claims.

The persons on whom the notice must be served are those who are required to convey, or join in conveying, an estate or interest in the land to the authority, and all persons who have such interest in the land as would enable them to interfere with the authority's possession of the land.

Section 30 prescribes the method of service. The notice may be served by delivering it to the addressee or by leaving it at his usual address, but if he is absent from the United Kingdom or cannot be found the notice may be left with the occupier of the land. If there is no occupier it may be affixed to the land. The First Schedule to the 1946 Act provides for an alternative procedure by way of registered post or recorded delivery and this is still available. Where the notice is to be served on a limited company it must be served upon the secretary or clerk to the company.

Effect of the Notice

It is important to note that a distinction must be drawn between a contract of sale, a notice to treat and a conveyance. These are three distinct and separate steps in an agreement. The notice to treat in itself does not create a contract of sale, for all the details have not been agreed upon sufficient to create a contract. Similarly the conveyance itself is not made – though once the price to be paid is agreed upon, after the notice is served, an obligation to convey the property arises: a contract to sell has then been created and the obligation can be enforced by specific performance. As Salmon L.J. put it:

> It is not until compensation is agreed or assessed that the equitable title in the land passes to the party who has served the notice to treat. Either party can then – but only then – obtain specific performance, the one to have the legal title conveyed to him on payment of the price, the other to have the price paid on conveying the legal title.[4]

Withdrawal of the Notice to Treat

Once a notice to treat has been served it can be withdrawn only in two circumstances:

(*a*) where the other party consents; or

(*b*) where withdrawal is permitted by some statutory power.

Statutory powers are contained in section 8 of the Compulsory Purchase Act 1965 and section 31 of the Land Compensation Act 1961. By section 31 an authority may withdraw a notice to treat within six weeks of receiving a claim for compensation; if the owner puts in no such claim the authority may withdraw the notice within six weeks of the Lands Tribunal determining the purchase price to be paid. Section

8 of the 1965 Act states that where an authority requires only part of a house, building or manufactory, or park or garden belonging to a house, and the owner is prepared to sell the whole of the property, the authority can be called upon to purchase the whole. If this happens the authority may withdraw the notice to treat.

Abandonment of the Notice to Treat

A notice to treat may not be withdrawn except under the circumstances already noted but it is possible that the rights given by the notice may be lost by abandonment. In *Simpsons Motor Sales (London) v. Hendon Corporation* (1962) the effect of the notice to treat was dealt with. The court stated that the service of such a notice conferred legal rights on both parties – on the acquiring authority the right to acquire the land on payment of proper compensation, and on the landowner the right to have compensation assessed and paid. Mere service of the notice gave no estate or interest in the land to the acquiring authority nor did it amount to a contract. But the rights noted were acquired. The Court of Appeal then went on to state the following propositions:

(1) When a notice to treat has been served it is the duty of the local authority to proceed to acquire that land within a reasonable time.

(2) The acquiring authority may evince an intention to abandon the notice to treat, and delay is some evidence of such an intention. A purported abandonment is wrongful and may be accepted by the owner of that land like the wrongful repudiation of a contract.

(3) The acquiring authority may act *ultra vires* by showing a continuing intention to acquire the land, but for a purpose not connected with the compulsory purchase order.

(4) Apart from delay or abandonment the parties may have so conducted (or misconducted) themselves in relation to the other that the other party may lose the right to enforce in equity the legal rights given by the notice to treat.

The House of Lords considered the matter again, on appeal, and added the following points, while upholding the Court of Appeal:

(a) While the court has no jurisdiction to interfere with the enforcement of a notice to treat on the ground that circumstances have altered since it was given, delay in proceeding with the notice will entitle the court to interfere.

(b) The court may interfere in its equitable jurisdiction to prevent an authority from enforcing its legal rights under a notice to treat, but only if to do so would be against good conscience because of bad faith or abuse of power by the authority, or an alteration of position by the owner making it unfair in the particular circumstances.

Lapse of the Notice to Treat

By section 4 of the Compulsory Purchase Act 1965 if a notice to treat has not been served within three years of the date on which the compulsory purchase order operates the order will lapse.

Conveyance

After service of the notice to treat the amount of compensation will be settled. When this is done the land will be conveyed to the acquiring authority. Where the parties refuse to take compensation, or refuse to convey, or where they cannot show title to the land or cannot be found, the position is governed by sections 5(3) and 9 and Schedule 2 of the Compulsory Purchase Act 1965: the purchase money must be lodged in court and a deed poll executed, vesting the land in the authority.

By section 23 of the 1965 Act all costs of vesting must be borne by the acquiring authority.

General Vesting Declarations

A quicker method of vesting the property in the acquiring authority is provided by the Town and Country Planning Act 1968. By section 30(2) and the Third Schedule to the Act general vesting declarations may be made. The acquiring authority executes the declaration in accordance with the Compulsory Purchase of Land (General Vesting Declarations) Regulations 1969; legal title to the land, which is the subject of a compulsory purchase order properly confirmed, will then pass to the acquiring authority on the date on which the declaration takes effect. Once it takes effect the authority is able to deal with the land in any manner it wishes – it may, for instance, resell the land without having to wait for title to be investigated or for completion of the conveyance. The former owner may claim compensation for the land so acquired, but he would be called upon to prove his title to the land in question.[5]

POWERS OF ENTRY

Normally purchasers of land are able to enter upon their property immediately after completion. Acquiring authorities who have served notices to treat may however, enter at an earlier stage: any time after notice to treat has been served the acquiring authority may serve a notice of entry to take effect not less than fourteen days after service. This provision is supplemented by special powers of entry under general vesting declarations, contained in Schedule 3 to the Town and Country Planning Act 1968.

Interest at a prescribed rate is payable on the purchase price as it is finally assessed, from the date of entry to the date of payment. When the acquiring authority takes possession of the land the claimant has a right upon request, by section 52 of the Land Compensation Act 1973, to an advance payment of 90 per cent of the agreed or estimated compensation.

Displaced Persons

It may be that the exercise of the acquiring authority's right to enter upon the premises after service of notice of entry has the effect of displacing persons from their homes.

Where persons are so displaced, either by the redevelopment of land acquired or appropriated for planning purposes, or by a requirement to discontinue an existing use of land or to remove buildings, and no other suitable residential accommodation is available for them on reasonable terms the local authority must secure the provision of such accommodation *before* they are displaced. This requirement does not apply in those cases where the persons in question have been dispossessed by the acquisition of land by highway authorities for roadworks.

It should be noted that the fact that a tenancy is a protected tenancy under the Rent Act 1968 does not mean that the tenant can prevent acquisition by the local authority. The authority has power to acquire possession of an occupied house on land required for planning purposes in spite of the protected tenancy status, provided the Secretary of State certifies that possession of the house is immediately required for the purposes for which it was acquired or appropriated.

Where persons carrying on business in any building on land acquired for planning purposes are displaced the Secretary of State or the local authority may pay such reasonable allowances as they think fit towards removal expenses and losses sustained by disturbance to the business. This topic will be touched upon again in the next chapter.

REFERENCES

1. Subject to certain provisos. The relevant sections are sections 214 to 225 of the 1959 Act and sections 44 to 56 of the 1971 Act.
2. The Code is found in the Third Schedule to the Act. There are certain other exceptions to the 1946 Act procedures; for instance acquisition under the New Towns Act 1965 and under the Pipe-lines Act 1962.
3. In *Lazarus Estates Ltd v. Beasley,* [1956] 1 Q.B. 702, p. 712.
4. *Birmingham Corporation v. West Midland Baptist (Trust) Association (Inc.),* [1970] A.C. 874
5. Section 11, Compulsory Purchase Act 1965; and see section 32, Land Compensation Act 1961.

8

Compensation

The matter of compensation may arise, in particular, in two important areas of activity in the construction industry. These are in planning and betterment, and in the compulsory purchase of land. These two may be dealt with separately.

COMPENSATION IN PLANNING MATTERS

In appropriate cases compensation is payable in respect of the refusal or conditional grant of planning permission; it may also be payable where planning permission is later revoked or modified. The main provisions are found in Parts VI, VII, VIII and XI of the Town and Country Planning Act 1971.

Planning Decisions Restricting Development

Various changes in the law occurred with the enactment of the Town and Country Planning Acts 1953 and 1954. All development value of land had been transferred to the State in 1947 and a general prohibition had been placed upon the carrying out of development unless a charge were paid to the Central Land Board. Compensation was payable to landowners for the loss of these development values, but the 1953 Act abolished the payment of development charges and cancelled the obligation to pay sums for lost development value. Since 1954, however, compensation can still be claimed where permission to develop land is refused, or where it is granted subject to conditions which are depreciatory in nature – but a claim under Part VI of the 1947 Act must have been established.

In effect this means that compensation will be payable if (i) the value of the claimant's land has been depreciated as a result of the local planning authority's decision, and (ii) the amount of the Part VI claim has not been wholly drawn on for other purposes: that is to say, there remains an 'unexpended balance of the established development value'. As already noted it will also be payable where planning permission is refused outright.

Unexpended Balance of Development Value. Land is taken to have an unexpended balance of established development value immediately after 1 January 1955 if there were then subsisting one or more claim holdings whose area consists of that land, or includes that land together with other land. The amount is calculated by taking eight-sevenths of the difference between the amount of any established claim and the amount (excluding interest) of any compensation paid (or set off against development-charge liability) in respect of acts or events occurring before 1 January 1955. This means, for example, that if compensation has been paid either by the Central Land Board or by a public authority there would be no unexpended balance. If only part of that compensation had been paid the unexpended balance of development value would be eight-sevenths of the amount remaining unpaid. Certificates in respect of these balances are issued by the Department of the Environment.

Assignment of such claims is recognised only where the assignment of benefit is shown to have been made before 31 December 1954.

Exclusion of the Right to Compensation. While the right exists as noted above, there are certain exceptions to the general rule. Thus a claim for compensation cannot be made:

    (*a*) where permission is refused for a change of use in an existing building;

    (*b*) where permission for the display of advertisements is refused, or granted subject to conditions;

    (*c*) where restrictive conditions are imposed, on a grant of planning permission, which relate to:

      (i) the number or disposition of buildings on the land;

      (ii) the dimensions, design, structure or external appearance of any building or the materials to be used;

      (iii) the manner in which the land is to be laid out;

      (iv) the use of any buildings or other land;

      (v) the location or design of means of access to a highway or the materials to be used for it; or

      (vi) the winning or working of minerals;

    (*d*) where permission to develop is refused on the ground that development is premature having regard either to the priorities indicated in the development plan for the area, or to deficiency in the provision for water supply or sewage;[1]

(e) where permission is refused because the land is liable to flooding or subsidence;

(f) where permission for any particular development is refused and there is available permission for development of a residential, commercial or industrial character, being development consisting wholly or mainly of the construction of houses, flats, shop or office premises, or industrial buildings (including warehouses).

In addition no title to compensation for planning decisions will arise where a public authority has acquired the land by compulsory purchase; where the public authority has appropriated land for a purpose for which compulsory purchase powers were available; or where land is operational land belonging to a statutory undertaker.

Procedure. Claims for compensation must be submitted on the prescribed form to the local planning authority for transmission to the Secretary of State. The claim must be made within six months of the planning decision unless the Secretary of State extends this period. Since the Secretary of State has power to review the decision of the planning authority and modify or substitute it he can avoid the payment of compensation by giving permission for development.

The amount of the compensation payable is based on the amount by which the value of the interest is depreciated by the decision as finally approved by the Secretary of State, or the amount of the unexpended balance of established development value immediately before the decision, whichever is the smaller.

If a claimant disputes the findings of the Secretary of State on compensation he may require the matter to be referred to the Lands Tribunal for determination. If the amount of compensation is in excess of £20 it is registrable as a land charge; notification must be given to the local authority and it should be registered in the local land charges register.

If the land is subsequently developed the Secretary of State may require the compensation to be repaid to him, but it was held in *Stock v. Wanstead and Woodford Borough Council* (1962) that if the details were not registered for some reason the repayment provisions do not apply. In *Ministry of Housing and Local Government v. Sharp* (1970) notice of compensation paid was entered in the register of local land charges but as a result of a negligent search by a clerk of the local authority later a certificate was issued stating the land was clear. The Secretary of State was unable to recover compensation paid from the purchaser of the land and he sued the local authority. The court applied the *Hedley Byrne* principle (see p. 26) and the local authority was found liable for the loss caused by the negligent search.

Modification and Revocation of Planning Consent

Where depreciation in the value of an interest in land has arisen as the result of an order which revokes or modifies a planning permission already granted, compensation is payable in respect of the full value of that depreciation, irrespective of whether there is an unexpended balance or not.

Compensation may also be payable where expenditure has been incurred in respect of work carried out after the planning permission which has now been rendered abortive by the revocation or modification of the planning permission. In such cases Exchequer contributions may be payable towards the compensation paid by local authorities.

As an alternative remedy a purchase notice may be served upon the planning authority if it can be shown that the land has become incapable of reasonably beneficial use in its existing state.

Restrictions or Refusals within Existing-use Development

Where the planning restriction or refusal relates to development falling within 'existing use' within the meaning of the Town and Country Planning Act 1971 (Part II, Schedule 8) a claim for compensation may be made under section 169 of the 1971 Act. Thus where the restriction applies, for instance, to the enlargement and improvement of buildings where the cubic content or gross floor space is not increased by more then one-tenth (or in the case of a dwelling by that amount or 50 cubic metres, whichever is the greater) an application can be made to the local planning authority for compensation to be paid. Compensation may be payable if the value of the land is shown to be diminished by the refusal or conditional consent, but the application for permission must have been dealt with by the Secretary of State, either by reference or on appeal.

Other Planning Restrictions

Compensation is payable for other planning restrictions in certain circumstances. These include:

(a) *Listed buildings.* Where the Secretary of State refuses consent to works of alteration or extension of listed buildings which either do not constitute development, or constitute development permitted under a development order, compensation may be claimed. It must be shown, however, that the value of an interest in the land is less as a result of the refusal.

(b) *Building preservation notices.* Compensation can be claimed for loss or damage caused by the service of such a notice, including loss for breach of contract caused by the necessity of discontinuing or countermanding works. It will be payable only if the notice ceases to have effect without the building being listed.

(c) *Authorised use.* If an order is made requiring the alteration or removal of a building, or which extinguishes an authorised use, compensation can be claimed for depreciation of the value of the interest in the land[2] and for disturbance in the enjoyment of the land. Alternatively a purchase notice may be served under section 189 of the 1971 Act if the land has become incapable of reasonably beneficial use in its existing state.

(d) *Tree-preservation orders.* Compensation may be payable for loss or damage caused by refusal of consent or imposition of conditions on a consent required under such an order, or by a direction to replant a woodland area felled under permitted forestry operations.

(e) *Stop notices.* Where loss or damage has arisen as the result of the prohibition contained in the stop notice and the enforcement notice has been quashed, or varied so as not to uphold the stop notice, or withdrawn (other than in consequence of grant of planning permission), or the stop notice itself has been withdrawn.

COMPULSORY ACQUISITION OF LAND

Where land has been acquired compulsorily the basis of compensation will vary according to the date on which the notice to treat was served. Where it was served between 1 January 1955 and 29 October 1958 the provisions of the 1954 Act still apply; where it was served between 30 October 1958 and 31 July 1961 the provisions of the 1959 Act apply. Compensation for land acquired where the notice to treat was served after 31 July 1961 is governed by the Land Compensation Act 1961. In effect the provisions are broadly similar.

Compensation arising from the compulsory acquisition of land may be of three kinds: it may be payable to the owner whose interest has been acquired, or it may be payable to the person whose interest is not acquired but prejudicially affected, or it may amount to a benefit for persons who have been displaced as a result of the compulsory acquisition. Separate considerations arise in the case of land acquired under Part III of the Housing Act 1957.

Compensation for Interests Acquired

The notice to treat served by the acquiring authority will have called upon the owner and other interested parties to submit particulars of claims for compensation. If the claims cannot be settled by agreement, or if no claims are made, the matter will be dealt with by the Lands Tribunal in accordance with principles laid down by statute. Loan sanction may be sought; in such cases Ministerial consent is necessary, and this will not be given unless the district valuer certifies that the purchase price of the land is in accordance with the statutory rules for the assessment of compensation.

The compensation will be made up of three elements:

(1) *Market value.* This is the amount which the land might be expected to realise if it were to be sold in the open market by a person willing to sell. It will take into account the use to which the land may be put, not merely its existing-use value. This general rule is, however, subject to certain modifications regarding the measure of compensation: see page 174. The effective date for the valuation was previously regarded as the value as at the date of the notice to treat, but it has been suggested that a more appropriate date would be that on which the acquiring authority takes possession, or when the purchase price is agreed, whichever is the earlier.

In applying the principle of market value certain assumptions must be made by virtue of sections 14 to 16 of the Land Compensation Act 1961. It should be *generally* assumed that:

(i) planning permission would be given for the development envisaged in the proposals of the acquiring authority in relation to the land;

(ii) planning permission would be given for development of any class specified in the 1971 Act, Schedule 8 ('existing use' development);

(iii) planning permission would be given for development in respect of which a certificate of appropriate alternative development has been issued by the local planning authority under Part III of the Land Compensation Act 1961.

With regard to (ii) above, if permission for 'existing use' development has been refused, or granted conditionally, and compensation is payable, permission will not be assumed (or will be assumed subject to conditions). Moreover if compensation has become payable under section 51 of the 1971 Act, requiring the removal of a building or the discontinuance of a use, there will be no assumption that permission would be granted for rebuilding or resumption of the use.

In addition to these general assumptions there are certain *special* assumptions that may be made. Thus:

(a) where land is included in a development plan and appears on the plan as intended for specified development, planning consent for that development will be assumed to be given;

(b) where the land is shown in the development plan as an area allocated primarily for a specified use, or for a range of two or more primary uses, it will be assumed that permission would be granted for any development, falling within the specified primary use or range of uses, for which permission might reasonably have been expected if none of the land in question had been proposed to be acquired;

(c) where land is to be made subject to comprehensive development and this is to be an action area for which a local plan is in force it will be assumed that planning permission would be given for any development falling within the range of uses allowed for the area. But it must be development for which planning permission might reasonably have been granted on the assumption

(i) that the area has not been defined as an area of comprehensive development and no particulars or proposals concerning any land in the area appear in the current plan, and

(ii) that no development or re-development already carried out in accordance with the plan has taken place, and

(iii) that no part of the land is proposed to be acquired by a public authority.

The special assumptions are on the basis that they are subject to conditions which might reasonably have been imposed, and indications in the current development plan that the development might be allowed to take place only at some date in the future.

If a structure plan and local plan is in force they will together provide the planning assumption. If only the structure plan is in force either that plan or the former development plan will be regarded as the development plan according to which gives rise to those assumptions as to the grant of planning permission which are more favourable to the owner.

It may be that the planning permissions that already exist and the assumptions to be made do not give sufficient guidance. In such a case the owner of the interest which is being acquired, or the acquiring authority itself, may make an application under section 17 to 22 of the 1961 Act to the local planning authority for a certificate of appropriate alternative development. This certificate will state the classes of development, if any, for which planning permission might reasonably have been expected to be granted if the land were not being acquired by the local authority. The applicant must specify the class or classes of development which he thinks appropriate and the local planning authority may issue a certificate for all or any of the specified classes, or for some other class or classes. The owner of the interest to be acquired has a right of appeal against the certificate to the Secretary of State, as does the acquiring authority.

The procedure involving certificates of alternative development is not available where the land to be acquired lies within an action area, or is in an area allocated primarily for residential, commercial or industrial purposes.

(2) *Severance and injurious affection.* By section 7 of the Compulsory Purchase Act 1965 damages by way of a claim for severance can be made where the value of the land that remains after compulsory acquisition is so reduced that its new value, taking compensation paid for the land into account, is lower than what had been its total value before the land had been severed. In addition, where works are carried out on the land and as a result the land left to the original owner is reduced in value, he may make a claim for injurious affection. Should the damage be caused by the wrongful use of statutory powers the remedy would be an action for damages or for an injunction or both.

(3) *Disturbance.* Where land has been acquired under a compulsory purchase order the compensation payable will include not only the market value of the land but also a sum to compensate for the personal loss that might have been imposed upon the owner by the enforced sale. An example is provided by *Harvey v. Crawley Development Corporation* (1957). Mrs *H* agreed to sell her house at an agreed price to the corporation; the price included legal costs and expenses incurred in moving her furniture, and having carpets and curtains adjusted for her

new home. She made an additional claim for 'disturbance' and expenses arising out of an abortive purchase of a new home and out of the actual purchase of a new home. The court held that she was entitled to the costs; an owner can claim all the loss sustained provided it flows from the compulsory acquisition, was not too remote, and was the natural, direct and reasonable consequence of the dispossession. In *Minister of Transport v. Lee* (1965) however, it was held that the costs of preparing negotiating and settling a claim are not amounts 'attributable to disturbance' made irrecoverable by section 143(1)(*b*) of the Town and Country Planning Act 1962 (and see page 179).

Under section 46 of the Land Compensation Act 1973 the compensation for disturbance may in some circumstances be assessed on the basis of complete extinguishment. If the claimant is over sixty years of age and occupies business premises with a rateable value not exceeding £2250 and does not wish to relocate the business, on his undertaking that he will not dispose of the goodwill or start another similar business within the area and within the limits imposed by the authority, compensation based on total extinguishment may be paid.

In *Hull and Humber Investment Co. Ltd v. Hull Corporation* (1965) it was held that the costs incurred in obtaining by appeal to the Secretary of State a certificate of alternative appropriate development, so as to enable the value of the land to be assessed on a higher basis, could not be claimed from the acquiring authority as compensation for disturbance.

Land Compensation Act 1961. By section 5 of the Land Compensation Act 1961 certain limits are placed upon the total amount of compensation payable where the Lands Tribunal fixes the amount. Thus, it is not only the market value of the land which will be used. In addition the following principles must be taken into account:

(1) No allowance is to be made on account of the fact that the acquisition is compulsory.
(2) The value of the land must be taken to be the amount which it might be expected to realise if it had been sold in the open market by a willing seller: but in *Wimpey & Co. Ltd v. Middlesex County Council* (1938) it was held that this could not include prospective profits that a building developer might make.
(3) Where the land is specially suited or adaptable for a particular purpose this shall not be taken into account if the purpose is one to which the land could be applied only in pursuance of statutory

powers, or for which there is no market apart from the special needs of a particular purchaser or the requirements of any authority possessing compulsory purchase powers.

(4) Where the use to which the land is put increases its value or the value of any premises on the land it will not be taken into account if the use could be restrained by a court, or is contrary to law, or is detrimental to the health of the occupants of the premises or to the public health.

(5) Where the land is (and if not compulsorily acquired would continue to be) used for a purpose of a kind for which there is no general demand or market the compensation may be assessed on the basis of the reasonable cost of reinstatement if the Lands Tribunal is satisfied that reinstatement in some other place is *bona fide* intended.

(6) The provisions of rule 2 above shall not affect the assessment of compensation for disturbance or any other matter not directly based on the value of the land.

Rule 5 was raised in *Edgehill Light Railway v. Secretary of State for War* (1956). The company whose land had been acquired by compulsory purchase claimed that the principle of equivalent reinstatement applied since no general demand or market existed for land of the kind they had; however, since there was no intention to rebuild the railway in another place the claim failed.

A claim also failed in *Festiniog Railway v. Central Electricity Generating Board* (1962) where the cost of reinstatement was found to be disproportionately high.

Sections 6 to 9 of the 1961 Act make it necessary for the Lands Tribunal to take certain matters into account, and leave other matters out of account, in applying the rules laid down in section 5. Thus:

(1) Account shall not be taken of an increase or decrease in the value of the land if it can be attributed to development or the prospect of development under a general scheme of development.

(2) If the owner of the land acquired also owns adjacent or contiguous land and the general scheme enhances the value of the land he retains, the amount by which the value is thus increased must be deducted.

(3) Depreciation in the value of the land must not be taken into account if it is attributable to the fact that an indication has been given that the land was to be acquired by a public authority.

Compensation for Persons Prejudicially Affected

Where a wrongful use of a statutory power occurs, or where negligence can be shown in the exercise of a permissive power, an action in tort might lie and damages may be claimed. The act in question must be one which would have been actionable at common law if undertaken by someone other than an authority acting under statutory powers, if an adjoining owner is to succeed in his claim for damages, but the underlying principles of payment for loss in such tortious instances is the same as that which is used in fixing the amount of compensation payable under statute. The *right* to compensation for an adjoining owner whose land is injuriously affected by the works carried out by the acquiring authority in the lawful exercise of its statutory powers is found in section 10 of the Compulsory Purchase Act 1965. This right was enlarged by Part I of the Land Compensation Act 1973.

Part I of the 1973 Act gives a right of compensation where, on and after 17 October 1969, the value of an interest in land is depreciated by physical factors caused by the use of highways, aerodromes and other works on land provided or used in the exercise of a statutory power. The physical factors are noise, vibration, smell, fumes, smoke and artificial lighting and the discharge on to the land of any solid or liquid substance.

If the persons affected have a right of action in nuisance at common law no claim can be made under the 1973 Act; it is available only where the common-law claim is debarred by statute. Persons able to claim the right to compensation are owners and occupiers of residential property, owner-occupiers of agricultural units and of other premises where the rateable value does not exceed £2250.

Restrictive Covenants. It is possible that the land acquired will be subject to restrictive covenants, such as that one which restricted the use of water found in the land in *Re Simeon and Isle of Wight Rural District Council* (1937). In that case the council had bought the land for the purpose of the water undertaking with the intention of building a reservoir. This would mean that the restrictive covenant was broken. The question arose whether the adjoining owner in whose favour the restrictive covenant ran could claim damages against the acquiring authority for breach of covenant. The court held he could not, though he *could* claim compensation. Effectively, therefore, the remedy in such cases lies under section 10 of the Compulsory Purchase Act 1965.

Displacement Provisions

Compensation may be payable for persons who have been displaced from their land as the result of the compulsory acquisition. Such compensation may be payable even if the persons concerned do not have a sufficient interest in the land to enable them to claim under the headings discussed above.

Home-loss Payments. Compensation may be claimed by a person displaced from his home as a result of a compulsory purchase order placed on the premises. It is equally payable as a result of displacement because of redevelopment by the authority or the making of orders under the Housing Acts such as clearance orders, demolition orders or closing orders. Before he can claim he must show the dwelling has been occupied by him as his main residence for five years previous to the order, etc. Caravan dwellers who have been displaced may also make claims unless an alternative site is provided for the caravan. In the case of blight notices (see page 167) home-loss payments cannot be made to the person serving the notice.

Authorities are compelled to make such payments for home-loss, but where the authority acquires by *agreement* even though it has compulsory powers the payment is then discretionary.

The amount payable is three times the rateable value of the premises subject to a maximum of £1500 and a minimum of £150.

Farm-loss Payments. Where a farmer has been displaced from the whole of his land as a result of compulsory acquisition of his interest he may claim a farm-loss payment provided:

(*a*) he owns the farm, or
(*b*) is a tenant with a term of years certain with not less than three years to run, and
(*c*) he begins to farm elsewhere within three years of the displacement.

The payment is discretionary where acquisition is by agreement under the shadow of compulsory powers; the amount payable is a sum equal to the average annual profit from the land acquired for a three-year period after deduction of a notional rent. If the compensation paid to the farmer for his interest includes development value and exceeds the existing-use value plus the farm-loss payment the farm-loss payment is not payable.

Disturbance Payment. A person who has been displaced from his land in the circumstances applying in home-loss payment situations can claim a disturbance payment unless he has a compensatable interest, but the payment is a discretionary one where there is no legal entitlement under these sections (37 and 38). The disturbance payment is made up of removal expenses and any loss (if any) occasioned by disturbance of trade or business as a result of the necessity to quit the land.

Rehousing. Under sections 39 to 43 of the Land Compensation Act 1973 housing authorities are placed under a duty to ensure that suitable alternative accommodation is available in cases of displacement from residential accommodation as a result of compulsory purchase orders, redevelopment or orders made under the Housing Acts. The duty does not arise where accommodation[3] is otherwise available on reasonable terms. Where it is a short-term tenant that is displaced the displacing authority may pay any reasonable expenses that he might have incurred, other than the purchase price for the acquisition of an alternative dwelling. The advance of a mortgage will discharge the rehousing obligation.

Compensation under the Housing Acts

Where property other than condemned property has been purchased under compulsory powers the assessment of compensation payable is based upon the same principles as those which were discussed above. They are made subject, however, to rules laid down in Part III of the Third Schedule to the Housing Act 1957. Thus no account may be taken of the fact that the letting value of the property has increased as a result of overcrowding or illegal use. Again account must be taken of disrepair of the property and of any appreciation in value to other premises belonging to the claimant because of the redevelopment or demolition.

Condemned Property. As a general rule it is only cleared site value which is payable as compensation, where an authority compulsorily acquires a house which is

   (i) unfit for human habitation, where it is included in a compulsory purchase order or is acquired as an individually unfit house, or

   (ii) declared to be unfit and incapable of being made fit by an order made by a local authority and confirmed by the Minister in accordance with the Second Schedule to the Land Compensation Act 1961.

The cleared site value will be the value of the site cleared of buildings and available for development, but it shall not exceed the market value of the site with the property on it. In *Davy v. Leeds Corporation* (1965) it was held that in assessing the site value account must not be taken of the clearance of adjoining property by the same order. The amount of compensation that may be claimed in respect of condemned property is affected by other factors, however, and in some cases the amount claimed may be greater than the cleared site value. This may happen in the following cases.

(*a*) *Houses used for business purposes.* Additional compensation may be claimed where the house which has been acquired at site value was used for business purposes, either wholly or partly. The person entitled to the receipts from the business may claim full compensation for his interest if he is the owner or tenant for more than a year, less the compensation for the site value. Such payments cannot be made unless the interest in the house was held on 15 December 1955 or at all times during the two years previous to the date of the compulsory purchase order.

(*b*) *Well-maintained property.* The Secretary of State may require the acquiring authority to make an additional payment in respect of the condemned house purchased compulsorily if he is satisfied after inspection by one of his officers that the property has been well-maintained over the previous five years. The payment will be made to the owner-occupier, or to the person responsible for the good maintenance and repair of the house if the owner is not in occupation. The payment may be shared where more than one person is liable for the maintenance. The amount will be four times the rateable value but cannot be greater than the difference between site value and full compulsory purchase value. The payments may also cover dwellings which have been *partially* well-maintained, in which case it will equal one-half the ascertained amount of the full payment. Payments at half the ordinary rate may be made in respect of individual dwellings in blocks of flats and in respect of property occupied partly for the purpose of dwellings and partly for other purposes.

(*c*) Where a dwelling is occupied by the owner, full compensation in accordance with the general rules of assessment will be payable provided certain conditions are fulfilled. These conditions are (i) that the dwelling has been occupied by the owner or a member of his family continuously since 23 April 1968, or (ii) it was acquired for occupation after that date and had been in owner-occupation for two years before the 'relevant proceedings' were begun (that is, before the declaration of the clearance area by the local authority). Where the owner-occupier satisfies the authority that he had made all reasonable inquiries before buying the property, and had no reason to believe that slum-clearance action would be started within two years of his purchase, he may claim payment of compensation even though the conditions noted above have not been satisfied.

(d) Both in respect of well-maintained and owner-occupier payments of compensation a guaranteed minimum payment is laid down. If the amount of compensation payable to the owner-occupier amounts to less than the gross value of the house it will be made up to the gross value.

Clearance, Closing or Demolition Orders. If an authority makes a clearance order, closing order or demolition order compensation is payable neither to the owner of property affected nor to its occupier. Payments may yet be made under the 'business premises', 'well-maintained' and 'owner-occupied' provisions mentioned above as they may in respect of disturbance allowances, dealt with on page 174. Thus, if a shopkeeper works in an area which is cleared he may be able to claim compensation for the loss he will now suffer as a result of the movement away of his customers, even though he cannot claim compensation for the loss of his property as such under the order.

Where property falls under the 'well-maintained' classification but is covered by a clearance order and is a condemned house the Secretary of State may call upon the authority to make an additional payment to the owner or occupier if he is satisfied after an inspection by one of his officers that the property has been well-maintained. In the case of closing orders or demolition orders any person may make representations to the authority, claiming that a 'well-maintained' payment should be made to him. If the authority refuses to make such a payment he may make an appeal to the county court.

Mortgage Relief. It may be that the owners of condemned houses have been buying the property on mortgage and outstanding liabilities remain. In such cases section 2 of the Housing (Slum Clearance)

Compensation Act 1965 has application. Section 2 extends the jurisdiction of the county courts under paragraph 5 of the Second Schedule to the Housing Act 1957 so that they may modify outstanding liabilities under mortgages or agreements to purchase by instalments as far as unfit houses condemned or compulsorily purchased are concerned. The section applies to owner-occupiers of all unfit houses, and in reaching its decision on modification the courts may take into account the extent to which the original purchase price of the house might have been excessive.

REFERENCES

1. Compensation will not be excluded on this ground if a further application is made after seven years have passed.

2. In accordance with section 5 of the Land Compensation Act 1961.

3. By section 42(1) it must be 'suitable' but this does not mean ideal, or identical accommodation. It is for the council to decide: *Savoury v. Secretary of State for Wales; The Times,* 10 Dec. 1974.

9
The Community Land Act 1975

The White Paper, 'Land' (Cmnd 5730), stated in September 1974 that the local administration of the proposals it made would require 12,750 extra staff, while the central administration would require a further 1400. This in itself militated against the immediate implementation in full of the principles enunciated in the Act which followed in 1975 – the Community Land Act.

The objective of the Act is to ensure that, with certain exceptions, no development will be allowed except on land that is owned by a public authority, or made available by the public authority for the purpose. Necessarily, this means that the authorities had to be given powers and placed under a duty to acquire land for such development, at current use value by agreement, or under compulsory purchase. The power included the right of the authorities to develop the land themselves or to make it available at market value for development by others.

RELEVANT DEVELOPMENT

The Act will bring development land into public ownership. 'Development' has the same meaning as in section 22 of the Town and Country Planning Act 1971 and covers both operations connected with land and the making of any material change in the use of buildings or land. 'Development land' is defined as land which in the opinion of the authority concerned is suitable for relevant development. By 'relevant development' is meant all development (except such classes as may be prescribed by the Secretary of State and all building of certain dwelling-houses which (a) are intended for occupation by the owner or a member of his family as his sole and main residence, (b) are freehold or leasehold with at least seven years to run vested in the owner on 12 September 1974, and (c) are subject to a claim for exemption by the owner). Classes exempted include: improvements, alterations and extensions to dwellings not involving a material change; certain enlargements of commercial buildings; certain developments on industrial sites and minor work such as the erection of gates and fences.

When the Act is fully operational its effect will be, as the Dobry

Report foreshadowed, that the nature and structure of planning control will have changed: no development will be allowed other than on land owned by a local authority or made available by it for that purpose.

The Act applies to England, Wales and Scotland and to a limited extent to Northern Ireland. The authorities in England are county and district councils, the Greater London Council, the Common Council of the City Corporation, new town corporations and the Planning Boards for the Peak Park and the Lake District. In Wales a special corporation will be set up: the Land Authority for Wales. It will deal with the acquisition of land and its management. It will have a duty to consult the county or district council in whose area the land is situated except where there is already a planning permission in force. In Scotland the authorities are the regional, general or district planning authorities or new town corporations.

DUTIES OF THE AUTHORITIES

Under the Act the authorities must first prepare a land acquisition and management scheme for the area of each county authority. In this way responsibility for the performance of functions under the Act will be allocated – to the authorities themselves, or to others. In preparing or revising the scheme the authorities must consider the resources available to the respective authorities and in particular the services of qualified and experienced persons, previous land acquisition experience, disposal and development, planning and local government law provisions, the other functions of the local authorities (especially housing) and such other matters as the Secretary of State may direct.

The scheme must include co-ordination arrangements and arrangements for dealing with disputes.

PLANNING, ACQUISITION AND MANAGEMENT

The fact that decisions have been taken in planning matters will not inhibit the operation of acquisition and management schemes. By section 17, though an authority must have regard to whether planning permission for a relevant development has been given or refused, a refusal *by itself* should not be taken as a determination that land is not 'development land' within the scope of the Act. Similarly, though the authority must have regard to any development plan, that plan itself is not to be seen as conclusive (though an amendment in parliamentary committee made it necessary under the Act for the authority to have regard to the development plan 'so far as material').

Thus, both in determining 'development land' and in acquiring such land, regard must be paid to the planning framework already in existence, as it must in relation to the declaring of 'disposal notifications' under section 25. Within the planning framework there must also be prepared rolling programmes of anticipated expenditure on the acquisition of development land, and these must be supported by such items as a regional (Government-endorsed) strategy, a structure or local plan, a development plan, or a non-statutory plan or policy adopted by the local authority. Similarly backed planning is also required in the acquisition of development land.

TIMING OF THE ACT

The operation of the Act is staged.

From the first appointed day authorities will consider the desirability of bringing development land into public ownership and are given power to acquire and dispose of development land.

From the relevant date in an order made under section 20 authorities are given the duty to acquire all land for designated classes of relevant development.

From the commencement date all planning permissions for relevant development are suspended on land which has not passed through public ownership.

The first appointed day powers will be exercised by the authorities by agreement, or, with the approval of the Secretary of State, by compulsory purchase. The authorities must take into account the needs of the inhabitants and business activities of the area, and the needs of builders and developers concerned in development in the area. They must also consider the needs and obligations of parish or community councils and statutory undertakers and such other matters as the Secretary of State directs.

If permission has been granted before the commencement date as a result of a planning application made after the first appointed day the authorities concerned must serve an acquisition notice under section 27 of the Town and Country Planning Act 1971 on the applicant and anyone else named in the certificate. Where the authority notifies (or is deemed to have notified) its intention not to purchase the land it is treated as having abandoned the intention to purchase. A presumption of abandonment arises also where notice to purchase is made but the first step towards acquisition is not taken within twelve months. Notice of intention not to purchase may be made subject to conditions. A notice may relate to part of the land if it is accompanied by an identifying plan.

Suspended Permission

By section 22 a planning permission is suspended until all authorities abandon purchasing power or an authority purchases the land – whichever is the earlier. If there is an abandonment, the authority loses its power to purchase compulsorily for five years or until breach of a condition. The power revives, however, at the end of the five-year period unless planning permission has meanwhile been implemented.

By section 21 a similar procedure applies to applications made before the first appointed day where permission was granted after 12 September 1974, provided notice of election is served on the owner or all authorities, or any of them. The notice must be served by the owner of a material interest – the freehold, or a lease with at least seven years to run – or a person who has entered into a binding contract to purchase such an interest.

When the Secretary of State makes a section 20 order the authorities in the area must arrange for all outstanding material interests to be acquired. This duty does not apply to land where the power has been abandoned under sections 21 or 22; land not needed for designated relevant development within ten years; land where a material interest has been disposed of by the local authority; or operational land of statutory undertakers.

From the commencement date all planning permissions granted for relevant development shall be automatically suspended, irrespective of when the application was made, except where the authority has disposed of a material interest in the land and the development is carried out by someone owning the interest or his successor in title, to whom the authority has issued a certificate stating its approval of the development in accordance with the planning permission. Thus, development by a private owner is possible only where the land has passed through the authority's ownership.

Enforcement action where development is carried out in spite of suspension of permission can be taken under Part V of the Town and

Country Planning Act 1971. The value of the development will be ignored in any subsequent assessment of compensation.

Where an authority decides that land should be made available for development by others it must have regard to applications to negotiate to carry out the development from:

(a) a person who owned a material interest in the land immediately before it was acquired by the authority;

(b) any person applying for planning permission for development of the same class for which the land is being made available and made concurrently with the planning permission application.

After having regard to such applications the authority must consider such other matters as the Secretary of State might direct.

THE EFFECT OF THE ACT ON PLANNING LAW

These radical changes envisaged in planning law will not be immediate. The duty to prepare land acquisition and management schemes *is* immediate but events must then await the fixing by the Secretary of State of the first appointed day. Only then will the authorities formulate their acquisition policies. The third step, the designation of development land by the Secretary of State, presupposes the prior existence both of relevant development and of the duty to consider acquisition policies which will have arisen on the first appointed day.

The practical effects of the Act can only be guessed at. The intention behind the Act is the provision of a more positive system of planning, but much will depend upon the methods of implementation used by the authorities. There is the fear, in addition, that the provisions of the Act will lead to a 'drying up' of planning permission applications from private landowners and developers, but perhaps of even more importance is the danger of conflict of interest, within the authorities, between planning and financial considerations. Amenity considerations may go out of the window in the face of the possibility of public profit.

COMPENSATION

Sections 27 to 29 deal with land compensation matters. Section 27 applies to compensation in respect of every compulsory acquisition of an interest in land (under the 1975 Act or any other) in pursuance of a notice to treat served on or after the second appointed day. In assessing the compensation payable it is assumed that planning permission *would not* be granted for any relevant development (except development which is not new development), and that in the case of suspended planning permission *has not* been granted. Additionally, no account shall be taken of changes in the kind of development effected after the second appointed day.

By section 28 where

(a) notice to treat was served on or after the appointed day,
(b) the person acquiring the interest is an authority or local authority in Wales or a Minister,
(c) the person from whom the interest is being acquired is an authority or a local authority in Wales,

the rules for assessing compensation shall be in accordance with section 5 of the Land Compensation Act 1961 (and section 12 of the Land Compensation (Scotland) Act 1963), subject to such modifications as the Secretary of State, with Treasury consent, shall make by regulations.

To consider cases of financial hardship arising in such compensation matters the Secretary of State may, by section 29, establish 'financial hardship tribunals' to which persons who claim they have suffered financial hardship as a result of the Act may apply. If the claim is justified the tribunal may make an additional payment to such persons. The specified amount must be paid by the authority liable to make the original compensation. The maximum amount such a tribunal may order to be paid is £50,000, though higher amounts may be prescribed by regulations. Such regulations, and those setting up the tribunals and conferring functions on them, must be approved in draft by Parliament.

Effect of the Compensation Provisions

The effect of these provisions is that nothing will be payable for prospective development value that relates to any 'relevant development', so market values of land will be held down, largely, to the existing use of land acquired. It should be noted that this change lies in a future when 'all areas in Great Britain are subject to one or more orders' prescribing a relevant date. When that time arises, if ever, the community land system will be in working order and the major steps in its implementation will have occurred.

EMPTY OFFICES

Part IV of the Community Land Act sets out a code for the compulsory acquisition of unoccupied office premises. By section 30 where the office accommodation comprises more than 5000 square metres and at least 75 per cent of the accommodation has remained unoccupied for at least two years the Secretary of State may acquire the premises by compulsory purchase.

The amount of compensation payable in such cases is the value of the interest assessed by reference to prices current on the date on which the erection of the office building was completed. A formula is laid down in section 31 but the effect of the provision is, broadly, that only the *lower* amount is to be taken of values current at the acquisition date and values current at the date of completion of construction. The Secretary of State may specify which date he wishes to apply as completion of construction (subject to right of appeal to the county court).

In the assessment of compensation for lesser interests such as leasehold reversions or mortgaged land or interests in part only of the property, the proportionate value payable is to be established by ascertaining

(*a*) the proportion of the value by reference to prices current at the later date;

(*b*) the full value to which that proportion relates (i.e. of the unencumbered legal freehold) by reference to price at the earlier date.

This cannot be done to the detriment of a mortgagee, however.

The effect is that changes in market value and alterations made to the premises during the interim period when the offices remained substantially unoccupied will be disregarded, by and large, unless they have the effect of lowering, rather than raising, the amount of compensation which is ultimately payable.

Index